DO IT RIGHT THIS TIME

I0152489

i

DO IT RIGHT THIS TIME

DO IT RIGHT THIS TIME

Overcoming the Obstacles to a Happy and Godly Marriage

DO IT RIGHT THIS TIME

DO IT RIGHT THIS TIME

MORAYO ISI

A PRACTICAL MANUAL FOR GETTING MARRIED TO THE RIGHT PERSON AT THE RIGHT TIME GOD'S WAY

DO IT RIGHT THIS TIME

Published by
Royal House Ministries
P. O. Box 420756,
Houston, TX 77242
(281) 965-6727

Printed in the United States of America

"The Lord gave the word: great was the company of
those that published it."
Psalm 68:10-12.

DO IT RIGHT THIS TIME

Special Dedication

This book is dedicated to the person of The Holy Spirit, who is the GREATEST Author of all ages. Not only is HE my BEST friend and CLOSEST ally but He is my STRONGEST critic. He teaches me what and how to write and then goes the extra mile and helps me to perfect it.

To HIM be glory, honor, and praise forever. Thank You my darling Holy Spirit. You are MARVELLOUS AND EXTRAORDINARY!!!

May You continue to reign in my life, my home, my ministry, my writing........

BOOKS BY MORAYO ISI

AUTOBIOGRAPHY

Turning Point

BIOGRAPHY

Amy A Sign and a Wonder
Amy A Sign and a Wonder: The Sequel

MANUALS FOR CHRISTIAN LIVING

The Wall Has Come Down
Seizing the Moment:
Walking through the God Opened Door
Do it Right This Time
Power to Shine
One Step Ahead
Behold I Do a New Thing
Oneness
The Mary Magdalene in Me
Remember Me O Lord
The Buck Stops Here
Deliverance or Discipline
The Great Provider
The Kingdom of God
Possessing Your Inheritance
Winning the Battle of the Bulge
Divine Settlement
Divine Compensation
Prayer Manual for Obtaining Your American Citizenship
Settle Me O Lord
The Unique World of Dreams
Dealing with Rejection
Destroying Evil Marital Yokes

CONTENTS

DO IT RIGHT THIS TIME

ACKNOWLEDGEMENTS

I give all glory to God Almighty, My All in All, who has called me to write, to teach, encourage, and exhort not only His body but even also the nations. He has promised me that my books will make an impact. They will be read in the nations of this world. My gratitude to the Holy Spirit who constantly teaches and guides me.

I also express my deep gratitude to various men and women of God that have sown into my life particularly my father in the Lord, and longtime mentor, Bishop Olu Itiolah, General Overseer, Fresh Anointing International Ministries, my father in the Lord Dr. D.K. Olukoya, General Overseer, Mountain of Fire and Miracles Ministries, and Pastor W. F. Kumuyi, General Superintendent, Deeper Life Bible Church, who gave me a sound spiritual foundation, and Pastor E. A. Adeboye whose devotional, Open Heavens, is a great treasure to me. Thank you Sirs. God bless you.

My gratitude to the members of Mountain of Fire and Miracles Ministries, Long Island, NY. Thanks for all your support. Special thanks to David Famuyide and his family. You have made all these possible. Special thanks to my daughter, Elewechi Osueke, who designed the original cover of this book. To my sister in law and fellow writer, Pastor Bridget Bazunu, I say thanks for always being available and there for me.

Last but not the least a very big thanks and love to my children for being my sampling board and for their love and encouragement.

I love you all very much. May the Lord God keep you and bless you always. Amen!!!

WHO CAN BENEFIT FROM THIS BOOK?

Among others, you will benefit from this book if:

- You desire to know the God prescribed way to get married.
- You mentor people who desire to get married in a godly way.
- You mentor people who are in troubled marital relationships such as marriage, sexual perversion, immorality and homosexuality.
- You desire to but are having problems getting married.
- You are lonely as no one from the opposite sex ever talks to you.
- You need guidance identifying and meeting your divine partner.
- You are confused or concerned about making a mistake in marriage.
- You believe that your marital life is cursed or bewitched.
- Your life is following the evil marital patterns of your family including divorce, polygamy, incest, and illegitimate babies.
- You are experiencing repeated disappointment by prospective spouses.
- Constant rejection, hatred, and jilting in marital relationships.
- Evil powers, and spirits, have decreed you will never marry.
- You know who you partner is but he/she is not interested.
- You are married to a spirit spouse, a snake, and other idols.
- You are experiencing satanic delay in getting married.
- You are usually attracted to the wrong people.
- You are constantly being used and dumped.
- You are married but have no joy or fulfillment in it.
- You are experiencing bad luck in your marital life.
- You cannot seem to get it right in the area of marriage.
- And Much More......!!!! ☺☺☺...

INTRODUCTION

Please sing this song with me:

> **When Jesus says yes**
> **Nobody can say no**
> **When Jesus says yes**
> **Nobody can say no**
> **When Jesus lifts you up**
> **Nobody can bring you down**
> **When Jesus opens the door**
> **Nobody can close it**

In 2006 while visiting a friend in Lagos, a city in Nigeria, West Africa, I fell asleep on the couch after our morning devotion. The music was playing on the radio while I slept. In my sleep, I had a life transforming dream which gave birth to this book.

In the dream, I found myself my spiritual father, Dr. Olukoya, the General Overseer of Mountain of Fire and Miracles ministries, Dr. D. K Olukoya. I had with me also a man who was apparently my God ordained Spouse. Dr. Olukoya was counseling us and all the time that he was doing so there was a particular song playing over and over in the background in the dream. I could hear it very clearly. It was titled "Do It Right This Time."

Dr. Olukoya told us that God in His infinite mercies and providence was giving us a second chance this time to do it right in the area of marriage. He said we were very blessed that God was giving us this second chance as we had both failed in our respective first marriages. Apparently both of us had been married once before and the marriages ended disastrously in divorce. He told us that this had done a great damage to our destinies. Again, he repeated that we were lucky to be getting a second chance at marriage as some people never get a second chance at marriage after failed previous marriages

Dr. Olukoya further counseled us that it was very important that we go about marriage the correct way this time. In other words, we had to "do it right this time," just like the song that was playing in the background kept saying. He said this was necessary because if we failed to do it right this time around, our destinies may never recover from another failed marriage. He emphasized that it was only because of the grace and mercy of God that we were being offered this second chance at marriage. He emphasized that some people are not as lucky as their destinies and their lives never even recover from a bad first marriage.

I was then asked to write a book on what had happened in the dream including the counseling that we got in the dream. The book was to be a manual on getting married the God way, at the God ordained time, and to the God ordained person and was to be titled "Do it right this time."

When I woke up from the dream, there was actually a song playing on the radio in the physical. It was titled "Do It Right This Time." However, unlike the song with the same title which played in the background in my dream, it was not about marriage, but about Nigeria, my country of birth. It talked about the need for Nigeria as a country to do it right this time. This song writer apparently wrote the song because Nigerians were being given another chance to change the destiny of Nigeria and change things around for good by choosing the correct leaders to run the country as it was election were holding April that year which was just around the corner. At this time the country was preparing for the 2007 Presidential elections. The music talked about the need for the government and the people to change their ways and to get it right this time around so that the country could move forward.

This book is the finished product of that encounter that I had with God in the dream described above and the mandate that I was given to write this book. This is because usually when you see men and women of God in a dream, it is God Himself talking to you using the faces of ministers that you know and trust to speak to you and give you a message. At other times they are ministering angels. **Hebrews 1:7, 14.** Therefore, my encounter with Dr. Olukoya in the dream was actually an encounter with the Living God concerning my marital destiny.

Having shared all, I have just a few more words to say to the readers of this book, a book that the Lord has told me will cut across international, national, racial, sexual, and other boundaries.

In the area of marriage, things may be looking impossible for you right now. Maybe you are asking yourself questions such as "How shall this whole marriage thing be?" "Why is my case so different?", "Why is it so difficult?"; "Will I ever truly be married?"; "Can I ever do it right in this area of marriage?" Today, I am here as a prophet of the Most High God, to tell you that though things may be looking bad right now, and everyone, including yourself, has given up on your getting married and actually enjoying it, you must refuse to give up and keep trusting God. God will settle you matrimonially. Marital bliss is possible and it is yours this season, in the name of Jesus. Receive it in the mighty name of Jesus.

Even if you have tried and fallen several times, you should never be afraid to try again. Failure is not when you fall but when you fall and refuse to get up and try again. Delay is not denial. History is full of people that fell but from the ashes of that fall they rose to the mountain top in various areas of their lives including marriage. Your case will not be different. In the area of marriage you shall arise and shine in Jesus name. You will make it. Arise and shine in the name of Jesus.

PRAYERS
1. I put my feet in the supernatural shoes of Jesus Christ. I will not fail or fall.
2. In the area of marriage, because of Jesus, I am a success not a failure.

You see, God knows what to do to make your blissful marriage to manifest by fire. He knows how to move your marital destiny forward and the right time to do so. He knows where your spouse is and can bring him or her to you and verse versa. Let us just acknowledge the awesome power of God to change our marital situation by singing this song loud and clear:

> **Jesus never fails**
> **Jesus never fails**
> **The men of the world may let you down**
> **But Jesus never fails**
> **Your father may let you down**
> **Your mother may let you down**
> **You pastor my let you down**
> **But Jesus never fails**

Sing the following song with me also:
> **I cannot fail**
> **I cannot fail**
> **Because of Jesus**
> **I cannot fail**

I prophesy over your life that in this all important area of marriage you shall not fail in Jesus name. Even if you have been failing before, receive your deliverance and your victory in Jesus name.

I am compelled to give a strong word of caution here. Please note that this is a prayer manual and not just another book. It is not a piece of literature that you just read and put away. It is not even a "regular" prayer book. It is a prayer, spiritual warfare, and deliverance manual given by the Holy Ghost for this hour for singles, divorcees, married couples, and others struggling in the area of marriage to recover their lost ground.

It is a spiritual warfare manual for acquiring the right spouse, God's way, and at the God appointed time. To use this book successfully, you have to put on a warrior mentality and be ready to fight for what is rightfully your inheritance as a child of Jehovah God. I know without a shadow of doubt that as you do that, the Warrior of all Warriors, Our Lord Jesus Christ, will arise and help you to win your marital battles. You shall overcome in Jesus name.

Always remember that marital fulfillment and joy are possible today. They are yours for the asking in Jesus name. In this book you will be taught and equipped on how to do this. It is a Do-It-Yourself manual that will teach you how to successfully get married and stay happily married.

REASONS FOR WRITING THIS BOOK

There are many reasons I have written this eye opening book at this particular time. It is given by the Holy Spirit for this hour to:

- Impart the revelation that the Holy Spirit gave to me in a dream concerning marriage. I was instructed to write it in a book and present it to the world. **Ephesians 1:7-8.**

- Equip singles with the right knowledge, skills, and tools to acquire a spouse God's way. **Isaiah 5:13; 2 Corinthians 10:5.**

- Expose the various obstacles and hindrances to getting married the God way and discuss how we can overcome them and move on to attain marital success and fulfillment. **1 Corinthians 16:9.**

- Damage the ignorance that is so prevalent in this area of finding and choosing the right spouse by exposing and eliminating the lies and misconceptions about marriage. **Hosea 4:6.**

- Inspire Christians and non-Christians from various backgrounds to experience the living God for themselves as the Master Matchmaker with whom nothing is impossible. **Luke 1:37; Luke 18:27.**

- Demonstrate the Lord God's ability not only to teach us how to relate to people of the opposite sex but also to help us to correctly connect to; identify; and choose the right mate. **Deuteronomy 29:29; Psalm 32:8.**

- To encourage the children of God to seek God and wait on His divinely ordained spouses for them and not just accept "anything" out of ignorance and desperation. **1 Corinthians 7:2, Isaiah 4:1.**

- Revive the broken and abandoned dreams of many of marital fulfillment and joy, and provoke a new awakening of hope, faith, and love in this very crucial area. **Proverbs 13:12.**

"I will not faint, for in due time and at the appointed season I shall reap, if I faint not." Galatians 6:9.

"Therefore do not cast away your confidence which has great reward. For you have need of endurance so that after you have done the will of God, you may receive the promise." Hebrews 10:35-36.

- To let everyone know that it is never too late to get married as God is the Restorer and the Master Matchmaker to the bargain. **Isaiah 3:14.** He knows how to redeem our wasted years and lost opportunities. This is particularly important for older brethren who may have given up hope of ever getting married.

  You should give up that kind of mentality and instead acquire the mindset and tenacity of Abraham. The Bible records that he waited for 25 years to have a child. Yet the Bible writing about him says that he never gave up on the prospect but kept hope alive until he had his heart's desire of the child that God promised him:

  "Who against hope believed in hope, that he might become the father of many nations according to that which was spoken, so shall thy seed be." Romans 4:18.

PRAYERS
1. I declare by the power in the blood of Jesus that this is my season to shine in the area of marriage.
2. Every power denying me of my right to get married, your time is up, fall down and die, in the name of Jesus.
3. I am a prophet, priest, and king. Every power denying me of my right to be king in any area of my life, die now, in the name of Jesus.

CHAPTER 1

WHY MARRIAGE IN THE FIRST PLACE?

God introduced the institution of marriage in the book of **Genesis,** which is the book of beginnings:

"And the Lord God said, It is not good that the man should be alone; I will make him an help meet for him. .... but for Adam there was not found an help meet for him. And the Lord God caused a deep sleep to fall upon Adam, and he slept: and he took one of his ribs, and closed up the flesh instead thereof; And the rib, which the Lord God had taken from man, made he a woman, and brought her unto the man. And Adam said, This is now bone of my bones, and flesh of my flesh: she shall be called Woman, because she was taken out of Man. Therefore shall a man leave his father and his mother, and shall cleave unto his wife: and they shall be one flesh." Genesis 2:18-24.

It is very important to point out here that even though there are many good reasons to get married, marriage is not for everyone. This is because God created everyone to fulfill a specific and peculiar purpose. For some the institution of marriage will not fit into the purpose of God for their lives. Therefore, you should first of all find out from God if He wants you to get married or if He wants you to live a single and celibate life devoted solely to Him and His work. **Matthew 19:12; 1 Corinthians 7:7-9.**

Several faithful servants of God in the Bible never married. This includes Jeremiah the prophet; Paul the apostle who wrote most of the

1

New Testament books in the Bible; and John the beloved who wrote the book of Revelation. As a single person with no immediate family to take care off, you are less distracted and can put more of your time and other resources into serving God. **I Corinthians 7:32-33.**

However, when God allows us, we should get married because the Bible contains several blessings and graces that a person derives from being married. Some are mentioned below while others will be mentioned later in the book.

TO FULFILL DIVINE DESTINY

"Before I formed thee in the belly I knew thee; and before thou camest forth out of the womb I sanctified thee, and I ordained thee a prophet unto the nations." Jeremiah 1:5.

God has a divine plan and purpose for everyone before He even creates them in their mother's womb. **Jeremiah 1:5, Jeremiah 29:11**. So everyone here on earth is on a divine assignment. Not only should you discover your divine purpose but you should marry someone who will help you to fulfill it. You should not marry anyone that will divert or take you away from it. For example, if the Lord has called you to be a minister but the brother is only interested in business and making money with no interest in serving God, then that is the wrong relationship for you. He will frustrate your calling. Therefore, you should marry someone that is going in the same direction as you not the opposite direction.

You should also be aware that the fact that a Christian brother or sister is available does not mean that he or she is your God ordained spouse. You should prayerfully find out who your correct partner is.

PRAYERS

1. Every agenda of darkness concerning my marriage, I bury you.
2. I refuse to marry my enemy in the name of Jesus.
3. Any power or personality manipulating me into a relationship that God has not ordained for me, fall down and die.

MARRIAGE BRINGS HONOR

A good reason to marry is that it commands honor. The Bible tells us in **Proverbs chapter 31**, that the husband of the virtuous woman is known at the gate and sits among the respected and influential in the land. It goes further to say that the works of the wife and the fruit of her hands brings her honor and distinction.

MARRIAGE ATTRACTS GOD'S FAVOR

Every woman will not make a good wife and not every man will make a good husband. However, a man that is able to secure a good wife will enjoy the favor of God:

"Whoso findeth a wife findeth a good thing, and obtaineth favour of the Lord." Proverbs 18:22.

MARRIAGE PREVENTS LONELINESS

"And the Lord God said, It is not good that man should be alone; I will make him a help meet for him." Genesis 2:18.

The scripture above tells us that right from the beginning of creation God instituted marriage to prevent loneliness and to provide companionship for man. God made man in His own image so He knew that man would crave fellowship just like Him. It was this craving that brought God daily to the Garden of Eden to commune with Adam. **Genesis 3:8**. So God made a mate for Adam to keep him company so that he would not be lonely. It is for this same reason of preventing loneliness and providing companionship that God sets the solitary in families. **Psalm 68:6.**

To alleviate loneliness, the word of God commands married couples to cleave to each other.

"Therefore shall a man leave his father and his mother, and shall cleave unto his wife: and they shall be one flesh." Genesis 2:24.

3

The Bible records that a major part of what Rebecca did for Isaac when she married him was to bring him companionship which helped him to get over the loneliness and grief caused by the death of his mother, Sarah. **Genesis 24:67.**

PRAYERS

1. Every covenant of ancestral loneliness delaying my marriage, break by fire, in the name of Jesus.
2. I bind and break every foundational yoke of loneliness causing problems for me in marriage.

MARRIAGE PROVIDES A HELP MATE

A good reason for marriage is that it provides one with a helpmate. We see this in the lives of Rebekah and Isaac. **Genesis 2:18, 23-25.** Both parties become one and bring into the relationship all their wealth, virtues, experience, potentials, connections, and other assets. This is because there is strength in numbers and that two are better than one. **Ecclesiastes 4:9.** They scratch each other's back; keep each other warm when it is cold; and help each other out. **Ecclesiastes 4:11-12.**

In the area of spiritual warfare, they are also better off also because they become each other's prayer partner. This is a good thing as the Bible says that one shall chase away a thousand enemies and two shall chase ten thousand. **Deuteronomy 32:30.**

MARRIAGE PROVIDES A CONFIDANT

"And Adam said, This is now bone of my bones, and flesh of my flesh: she shall be called Woman, because she was taken out of Man. Therefore shall a man leave his father and his mother, and shall cleave unto his wife: and they shall be one flesh." Genesis 2:23-24.

In getting a divinely ordained spouse, you get a confidant with whom you can share intimate and confidential things without being bashful or concerned that the information may end up in the wrong hands as is so often the case in marriages these days. This is reinforced in the Bible

4

which says that a couple should not do anything that will hurt each other because when you do so, you actually hurt your own self. **Ephesians 5:28-29.**

The Bible says that Adam and Eve were naked and not ashamed.

"And they were both naked, the man and his wife, and were not ashamed." Genesis 2:25.

This means that they were on the same page and were knitted together as one spirit. It means that they were open with each other about the issues of their lives and did not hide behind cleverly fabricated facades. They could afford to be vulnerable with each other knowing that they are in safe hands and would not get hurt. This is why the Bible asks the question, "Can two walk together except they be agreed?" **Amos 3:3.**

Perfect love drives away fear the Bible says. **1 John 4:8.** So in a godly marriage, you should be able to be yourself and to open up your life to your partner without hiding skeletons in the closet. You should not have to hide behind a clever and false façade. How long can you sustain that? It should also not be the case of one person opening up their life while the other one hides everything. Some even prefer to share things with their family members and hide these things from their spouse.

The Christian marriage is a joining of two individuals by the Holy Spirit such that there is no room left for two individuals but one. **Ephesians 5:31.** You should not even try to figure this out but allow the Holy Spirit to do His work in the union because the Bible clearly says that it is a mystery. **Ephesians 5:32-33.**

PRAYER

Holy Spirit, glue me and my God ordained partner together in such a way that nothing can separate us, not power, personality, or spirit, in the name of Jesus.

TO POPULATE THE WORLD

"Be fruitful, and multiply, and replenish the earth, and subdue it."
Genesis 9:1.

From the scripture above, God purposed marriage to populate the earth so that the human race can continue to perpetuate itself and not go extinct. Therefore, a good reason for getting married is procreation. This is necessary because God carries out His agenda on earth through men. It takes the presence and power of God to carry out the agenda of God. The presence of God can only be carried on the shoulders of men.
Numbers 4: 15.

King David learnt this truth the hard way when he tried to carry the ark of God which represented God's presence, on a wooden cart, instead of on the shoulders of men as required by God. In the process of doing so, God killed Uzzah, the priest, who drove the cart. **2 Samuel 6:6-7.**

God needs men on earth, to carry His presence, implement His agenda, and display His glory. A God ordained marriage is the acceptable means of producing men and women to carry out this divine assignment of procreation.

TO PREVENT IMMORALITY

The word of God warns us that it is better to marry than to burn with passion and unbridled unfulfilled desire for sex.

"But if they cannot contain, let them marry: for it is better to marry than to burn." 1 Corinthians 7:9.

It also counsels that getting married will prevent a person from falling into the demonic trap of fornication which is sex outside of marriage.

"Nevertheless, to avoid fornication, let every man have his own wife, and let every woman have her own husband." 1 Corinthians 7:2.

Pray the following prayer with holy anger:

Every sexual snare set for me, I jump over you, catch your owner.

TO PROVIDE A PROPER COVERING FOR THE WOMAN

A godly man provides the proper covering for his wife. A godly marriage is the vehicle for getting this kind of covering. This is because your husband or your divine partner is your covering. **1 Corinthian 11:15, Isaiah 4:1**. This is why any dream about hair being cut or shaved and hair covering such as scarves and hats being stolen, blown away, or lost should be taken very seriously. You should fast and pray to recover them back because failure to do so could adversely affect your marital destiny especially the relationship that you are in currently.

The man is indeed the covering of the woman because regardless of what the unbelievers say, there are many things that a man can do that a woman cannot do hence the Bible refers to her as "the weaker sex." **1 Peter 3:7.**

PRAYERS TO RECOVER YOUR MARITAL COVERING

1. Every power delaying my marital destiny, die now.
2. Every witchcraft agent that has stolen my marital covering, return it and die.
3. Every power struggling with me for my marital covering, release it, die.
4. Every power using my glory to shine, release it by fire.
5. Every power, spirit, or personality sitting on my marital glory, be unseated by fire.
6. Every power contending for my marital glory, your time is up, fall down and die, in the name of Jesus.
7. By fire, by force, I recover back my marital covering that has been stolen, exchanged, or lost, in the name of Jesus.

CHAPTER 2

WHAT DOES IT MEAN "TO DO IT RIGHT THIS TIME"?

There is a godly, biblical way to get married and there are also worldly and even outright demonic ways of getting married. The Bible talks of the way that seems right unto a man but which ends in death. **Proverbs 14:12.** It also talks about the narrow way, the way of God that leads to fulfillment and the broad way of the world that leads to destruction. **Matthew 7:13.** Our Lord Jesus Christ observed that not everyone will choose to follow the biblical principles that lead to abundance in various areas of life including marriage:

"But he said unto them, All men cannot receive this saying save they to whom it is given." Matthew 19:11.

As far as marriage is concerned, to "Do it right this time," means to get married to the God ordained person, at the God ordained time, and in the biblical way. It means that regardless of how you have done it in the past, now you can do it the right way, which is the way prescribed by God.

This is necessary because everything that a genuine child of God does should follow what is written in the Bible, which is God's manual for our lives. Ignorance is no excuse. It is our responsibility to find out what the Bible teaches on getting married the God way and to pattern our marital life after it without deviating. This will prevent us from doing it the wrong way which has terrible consequences.

This book will help us to do that. It is a do it yourself manual that will equip and give you a fresh opportunity to do it right this time around.

Doing it right this time means allowing God's perfect will to be done in your marital life as opposed to His permissive will, your own will, or the will of others. It means allowing God to bring the right people your way and then allowing Him to choose the correct spouse for you. This is God is limitless but we as humans are limited and do not possess enough wisdom or information on our own to pick the right spouse for ourselves. There is no way that you can know if the man is a murderer or if the woman comes from a family with a history of insanity, witchcraft, or divorce. God alone knows because He knows all things.

"Neither is there any creature that is not manifest in his sight: but all things are naked and opened unto the eyes of him with whom we have to do. Hebrews 4:13.

Doing it right this time entails knowing that marriage is a process involving many steps which are spread over a period of time. Doing it right means allowing God to guide you through these steps that lead to a godly marriage one step at a time. The process starts with praying to find out God's will for you in marriage and ends when you actually get married in a Holy Ghost filled church. Skipping any of these steps is a recipe for disaster as you could end up with a bad marriage.

Doing it right requires that you allow God to prepare you emotionally, mentally, spiritually, and physically for marriage. It entails allowing Him to guide you into the right relationship; through courtship; into marriage; and beyond.

"In all thy ways acknowledge him, and he shall direct thy paths." Proverb 3:6.

This is necessary because only God knows all things. He knows the heart of every man. He also knows what the future holds for you and His ordained spouse for you. He knows the end from the beginning.

Doing it right this time means seeking God in prayers and fasting to get the divine blueprint for your marital destiny. God has a purpose for every marriage and the blueprint to achieve that purpose. God is very specific when dealing with His children. He still speaks today and He expects His children to hear Him clearly when He speaks. **John 18:37**. He will show you who your spouse is and give you clear specific details about your marriage if you ask Him. You should write the information given to you down and pray them into manifestation as the vision is for an appointed time. **Habakkuk 2:3.**

Doing it right this time means observing divine timing. The Bible says that there is an appointed time for everything in life. **Ecclesiastes 3:1-8**. Doing it right means getting married at the God appointed time and not one minute earlier or later. This is necessary because marriage is a process and each step of the process has a time element attached to it. Therefore, like the children of Issachar, you should know God's times and seasons for your life and marriage. **1 Chronicles 12:32.** Missing your divine timing has adverse consequences as it may make it more difficult if not impossible to get married thereafter.

As we wait expectantly for God's appointed time for our respective marriages you can sing the following chorus with me:

> **In His time, in His time,**
> **He makes all things beautiful in His time.**
> **Lord, please show me every day**
> **As You're teaching me Your way**
> **That You do just what You say**
> **In Your time.**
> **In Your time, in Your time**

It is very important to marry the right way this time around because marriage affects every area of a person's life. A bad choice in marriage can slow down or destroy your destiny altogether. Realizing this, King Solomon, whom the Bible refers to as one of the wisest men that have ever lived wrote:

"Who can find a virtuous woman? For her price is far above rubies. The heart of her husband doth safely trust in her, so that he shall have no need for spoil. She will do him good and not evil all the days of her life." Proverbs 31:10.

CHAPTER 3

ARE YOU DOING IT THE WRONG WAY?

If there is a right way of getting married, then surely there is a wrong way of doing it also. Doing it the wrong way is to get married in a way that is not allowed in God's word or pleasing to Him. It is to do it the way that the unbelievers around you do it. It is to do it according to the pattern demanded by your family idols and their priests. It is to do it the way that your ungodly parents say.

This actually leaves you worse off than if you had not married at all but remained single, walking in the ways, counsel, and timing of God. It is an invitation to a lifetime of sorrow, tears, and regrets. We will now look at some of the ways that you can get married the wrong way.

You are not doing it right when you jump into a relationship without finding out from God if it is His will for you because you are too lazy to pray and ask God. It is just as bad to marry a Christian brother or a sister just because he or she is available without finding out from God if he or she is His choice for you in marriage.

You are not doing it right when you marry a man because you got pregnant for him out of marriage. This is regardless of whether he turns out to be God's chosen partner for you or not. This is because a bad foundation has already been laid for the marriage as the marital bed has already been defiled:

"Marriage is honourable in all, and the bed undefiled: but whoremongers and adulterers God will judge. Hebrews 13:4."

11

The same also goes for a man marrying a girl just because she got pregnant for him. It is a recipe for marital suicide and disaster.

The way of repentance is to let her have the baby and then prayerfully seek the Lord to see if she is really God's divine choice for you in marriage or not. If she is not, it would be unwise to rush into marriage simply because a child is involved. This is because God's plans for your life should supersede your own plans or what others think or say about you. You should both submit totally to our Lord Jesus Christ, the Master Mechanic, and let Him mend your lives. It is better to face reproach now than to face a life time of sorrow, tears, and regret.

Saying "I do" to please your family or because your friends are getting married and you want to be like them is certainly not doing it right. In the same token, marrying just to get away from an oppressive family life is doing it the wrong way. Instead, you should confront your family problems prayerfully, asking God to intervene.

Doing it right, demands that we should not be unequally yoked with unbelievers.

"Be ye not unequally yoked together with unbelievers: for what fellowship hath righteousness with unrighteousness? and what communion hath light with darkness? And what concord hath Christ with Belial? or what part hath he that believeth with an infidel? And what agreement hath the temple of God with idols? for ye are the temple of the living God; as God hath said, I will dwell in them, and walk in them; and I will be their God, and they shall be my people. Wherefore come out from among them, and be ye separate, saith the Lord, and touch not the unclean thing; and I will receive you. And will be a Father unto you, and ye shall be my sons and daughters, saith the Lord Almighty." 2 Corinthians 6:14-18.

Marrying an unbeliever or an immature Christian that will quench your fire is being unequally yoked and is not doing it right. An unbeliever is anyone that has not accepted the Lord Jesus Christ as his or her personal Lord and Savior. As Christians, our way of life should conform to Christ and the principles laid down in His word and not the world. **Roman 12:2.** We are not allowed to do things like the unbelievers around us. To do so is to become a de facto enemy of God as the Bible clearly says that friendship with the world is enmity with God. **James 4:4**

Becoming one of the wives of an already married man in a polygamous relationship is not doing it right. The same goes for polyandry, which is a woman marrying more than one man concurrently. The Bible only allows one man and one woman in a godly marriage.

"And he (Jesus) answered and said unto them, Have ye not read, that he which made them at the beginning made them *male and female*, and said, For this cause shall a man leave father and mother, and shall cleave to this wife; and they twain shall be one flesh? Wherefore they are no more twain, but one flesh. What therefore God hath joined together, let not man put asunder. They say unto him, Why did Moses then command to give a writing of divorcement, and to put her away? He saith unto them, Moses because of the hardness of your hearts suffered you to put away your wives: but from the beginning it was not so. And I say unto you, Whosoever shall put away his wife, except it be for fornication, and shall marry another, committeth adultery: and whoso marrieth her which is put away doth commit adultery." Matthew 19:4-9.

Regardless of what secular laws and the customs of this world allow, "marrying" a person of the same sex is not doing it right. The scripture above clearly says "Male and female." God destroyed the people of Sodom and Gomorrah for this very reason. **Genesis 13:13, Genesis 19:24-29.** The principles and values of God are eternal and do not change. As Christians, we are told not to conform to the standards of this world. **Romans 12:2.** The Bible endorses marriage between one man and one woman only and not between John and Mark or Mary and Jane. Instead of trying to rewrite the unchangeable word of God we should acknowledge that we have a problem. Then we should humble ourselves and ask God to help us deal with the problem, rather than justifying our desire for people of the same sex. **1 Peter 5:5-10.** He is ever available and willing to help if we come to Him. **John 6:37.**

Getting married through a dating or matchmaking service is pathetic and not doing it right. Let God do the matchmaking for you instead.

13

Invest the time wasted on doing this fruitless exercise in seeking God in prayers for your marriage instead. Just try it and the result will surprise you.

The Holy Spirit is the greatest Matchmaker in the universe. Moreover, unlike the world's dating system that is fraught with errors, mistakes, and mismatches, the Holy Spirit never makes mistakes. **Isaiah 34:16.** Ask Him to connect you to your divine partner.

Marrying a person just because you are from the same country or tribe is not doing it right. Asking your family back in your village to package you a person that you do not know and have never even met to be your spouse is certainly not doing it right. In fact, it is absolute madness.

As a Christian, being a member of the family of God should supersede all other relationships including all physical blood and tribal ones. Jesus redefined the human concept of family by saying that His family members were not His earthly mother and siblings, but anyone that keeps God's commandments and knows the will of God and does it. **Matthew 12:46-50.** You should use the same standard when picking a spouse.

If as a Christian, you go outside of God's family to marry, you are looking for trouble. This got several people in the Bible, including Samson and Solomon, in big time trouble. You can be sure it will get you in trouble as well. **Judges 16:1-31; Nehemiah 13:23-27.**

Marrying a woman because she is rich or telling your people in one of the third world countries to send you a medical personnel such as a doctor, nurse, or pharmacist as a wife because they easily secure high paying jobs in Europe and America is not acceptable. She is not a cow to be milked for money. You will end up becoming her Ahab and she your Jezebel, who manipulates, dominates, oppresses, and strips you of your manhood. You should refuse to be a victim. Please pray these prayers:

1. **O Lord, help me so that the stronghold of Jezebel will not make me to lose my chance of doing it right this time in Jesus name.**
2. **I challenge every spirit of Ahab in my life with the fire of the Holy Ghost, come out and die by fire, in the name of Jesus.**

DO IT RIGHT THIS TIME

In our bid to do it right this time, we should be like Abraham who refused to pick a wife for his son Isaac from among his idolatrous Canaanite neighbors. **Genesis 24:1-67.** He knew that would be a recipe for trouble and satanic diversion of all the great things that God had promised him and his descendants.

Today, as you too choose to do it right this time, I prophesy into your life the miracle of recognition and divine connection to your God ordained spouse. I pray that all the barriers that are separating you from your divine partner will be removed. I pray that the eyes of your God ordained spouse will be opened so that he can see that you are his (and so that she can see that you are hers) in Jesus name. I prophesy over your life that you are next in line for a miracle. The joy of marriage is yours. Receive your miracle in the name of Jesus. I prophesy over you that before this year is over you shall march down the aisle for your wedding singing the popular African wedding song:

> **You are the one**
> **I've been waiting for**
> **You are the one**
> **You are the one**
> **You are the one I've been waiting for**
> **You are the bone of my bones**

CHAPTER 4

SEVEN CONDITIONS FOR DOING IT RIGHT THIS TIME

There are conditions that should be met before a relationship can be said to be following the biblical pattern set by God in the Bible for getting married. These conditions are the minimum requirement that should be present for a relationship to qualify as a Christ centered relationship that will lead to a godly marriage. We will mention seven key conditions here.

1. MAKE GOD YOUR FRIEND

The first condition is to get to know God and become His friend. This can only be done through salvation through Jesus Christ. It is important to know who you are in Christ before trying to develop any other relationship whether marital or others. This is because knowing who you are in Christ will determine what relationships you enter into and the depth of such relationships.

Above all, God desires your friendship and communion. When you become God's friend every other thing including a godly marriage falls into place. **Matthew 6:33. (Please see the steps to becoming a friend of God in the appendix section of this book).** As you fellowship with Him, He will reveal secrets to you that will move your marital life to a height that you never dreamed off. **1 Corinthians 2:9.**

The song writer summed it all up when she said that there is truly no one greater than Jehovah. He is a loving Father that wants the best for His children. He is the only one that can help you to make the right choice in marriage because He is the only one that knows all things. He

16

has all the information that you need to pick the right spouse. Knowing Him is the greatest thing that can happen to a person. It influences every other area of a person's life including choice and depth of relationships.

God is the Master Matchmaker and Builder when it comes to marriage. **Genesis 2:18.** The very institution of marriage originated from Him. Today, you must make God your friend and allow Him to secure the right spouse and marriage for you. Not only will He secure the right marriage for you, but He will also help you to build it:

"Except the Lord build a house, they labor in vain that build it: except the Lord keepeth the city, the watchmen waketh in vain." Psalm 127:1.

From the following examples from the Bible, we can see that it is in our own interest to do so.

The patriarch Abraham made God his friend and at his request, God provided a good wife for his son Isaac. **Genesis 24:1-67**. Today, as you too make Him your friend, God the Master Matchmaker will bring you the spouse that He has custom designed just for you like He did for Isaac and for Adam. **Genesis 2:21-22.** He will also build you a wonderful home to the bargain, in Jesus name. Amen.

The Bible also records for our example the lives of two non-Hebrew women, Ruth and Rahab. Their decision to make God their friend paid off for them wonderfully in marriage.

Ruth was a widow, who had lost everything including her husband, family, and home land. Unlike her sister in law Orpah who chose to return to her people and to her idols, she made a bold decision to stick with her beloved mother in law Naomi and to make Naomi's God her God.

"And they lifted up their voice, and wept again: and Orpah kissed her mother in law; but Ruth clave unto her. And she said, Behold, thy sister in law is gone back unto her people, and unto her gods: return thou after thy sister in law." Ruth 1:14-15.

This singular decision changed her life forever and rewrote her history. It transformed her life from that of a victim to that of a victor and turned her into a bundle of testimonies. God restored her by giving her a husband of great honor and wealth, Boaz, who became the father of her son, Obed. **Ruth 4:8-22.** Even today her story is still being told and her testimony shared. I pray that generations to come will share your marital testimony as well in Jesus name.

The case of Rahab, the harlot, is an even more outstanding example of God's mercy and His desire and ability to take care of His friends. She befriended and helped the Israelites, God's people, in their time of need. In return, they rescued her and her family from destruction. **Joshua 6:23-25.** As if that testimony was not enough, she eventually married Salmon, a man of honor and distinction among God's people, the Israelites.

Through these two divinely orchestrated marriages, God positioned Ruth and Rahab to become the ancestors of our Lord Jesus. Their stories are written for our example in both the Old and New Testament books of the Bible. **Matthew 1:5; Hebrew 11:31**. Even so shall our God ordained and orchestrated marriages distinguish us and catapult us locally and globally to honor, distinction, and recognition in our generation in Jesus name. Our marriages will indeed announce us to the world in Jesus name. Amen.

2. SEEK GOD'S DIRECTION FOR YOUR MARRIAGE

"I will instruct you and teach you in the way which you should go: I will guide you with my eyes. Be ye not as the horse, or as the mule, which have no understanding: whose mouth must be held in with bit and bridle, lest they come near unto thee." Psalm 32:8-9.

"And thine ears shall hear a word behind thee, saying, This is the way, walk ye in it, when ye turn to the right hand, and when ye turn to the left." Isaiah 30:21.

As redeemed children of God, divine direction and guidance are our covenant rights. Our Lord Jesus affirmed this by saying that His sheep hear His voice and will not listen to or follow any other voice. **John**

10:16, 27; Isaiah 30:21. The Bible also says that God will order our steps. **Psalm 37:23.** It is therefore very important to seek God's direction and will for your marriage. It is in our best interest to let Him show us and lead us to whom He has ordained for us to marry as He has promised to do in His word:

"I will instruct thee and teach thee in the way which thou shalt go: I will guide thee with mine eyes." Psalm 32:8.

There are many reasons that we should allow Him to do this for us.

First and foremost, God is the Alpha and the Omega who knows the end of a thing from the beginning hence the Bible says that He is:

"Declaring the end from the beginning, and from ancient times the things that are not yet done, saying, My counsel shall stand, and I will do all my pleasure." Isaiah 46:10.

So He knows what the end of any relationship will be before you even start it. He knows who you will marry and it will end well. He also knows who you will marry and it will end disastrously. Why not let Him direct you into the right relationship this time around? Do you not think that you have blundered enough trying to do it on your own?

Secondly, God can see everything that happens in the universe and also knows all things. The Bible tells us that nothing is hidden from Him:

"Neither is there any creature that is not manifest in his sight: but all things are naked and opened unto the eyes of him with whom we have to do." Hebrews 4:13.

He knows everything about you, including your thoughts, intentions, and motives. He knows the things that you hide from people. He even knows things about you that you do not know about your own self. So this puts Him in a better position than you are to choose the correct spouse for you. Allow Him to do so.

Thirdly, God does not want us to live our lives independently of Him or to depend on people. **Psalm 118:8-9.** Instead He wants us to depend on Him and to ask for His help and direction in every situation that comes our way including marriage.

"And I say unto you, Ask, and it shall be given you; seek, and ye shall find; knock, and it shall be opened unto you." Luke 11:9-13.

All you need to do is involve Him and He will show you things to come concerning your marriage and help you to acquire the right spouse, at the right time, and in the right way.

"Call unto me and I will answer thee, and show thee great and mighty things which thou knowest not." Jeremiah 33:3.

Please note that He is never late or early but always just on time.

Fourthly, God only wants the best for us in every area of life including marriage.

"For I know the thoughts that I think toward you, saith the Lord, thoughts of peace, and not of evil, to give you an expected end. Jeremiah 29:11.

"I am the Lord thy God which teacheth thee to profit, which leadeth thee by the way that thou shouldest go." Isaiah 48:17b.

The Bible provides a great example of God guiding a person into the correct marriage in the way that Abraham got a wife for his son Isaac. Abraham sent his servant Eliezer back to his country of birth to get a wife for his son Isaac. In sending him off, Abraham prayed for him for divine guidance in carrying out the assignment. **Genesis 24:7.** The servant also prayed for divine guidance throughout the journey. He specifically asked God to signify His choice of wife for Isaac by making her offer to fetch water for him as well as his camels to drink. **Genesis 24:14.** God answered his prayers because Rebecca came along even before he finished praying and at his request offered to fetch water from the well for him and his camels to drink. **Genesis 24:12-20.** Not only that, she turned out

20

to be from the family that Abraham had specifically sent him to get a wife from. **Genesis 24:23-27.**

Having seen what a marvelous God we serve in the preceding example, why not give God a chance and let Him guide you? Just like Abraham's servant, you will not be disappointed. As you inquire of the Lord through prayers, He will lead you speedily and directly to His spouse for you without any confusion and delay in Jesus name.

However, you should be aware that the person that God chooses for you may not fit the picture that you have of your spouse. Do not despair but trust God because with time God can make that person exactly what you desire in a spouse. He alone knows all things, so trust His impeccable judgment to guide you to the best for you in marriage. **Jeremiah 29:11.**

The Bible says that many are the plans of a man for his life but that only God's counsel will prevail. **Proverbs 19:21.** Therefore, you should not run ahead of God. Let His counsel alone stand in your life in this all important area of marriage. If there is no clear indication from Him to go ahead then you should wait. Pray for more revelation and proceed only if and when the Lord tells you to. Waiting includes not taking phone calls or seeing each other under various guises such as praying together, studying together, and fasting together. If you do, you will only get your fingers burnt and live to regret it. The Bible warns seriously about this in the scripture below:

"Can a man take fire in his bosom and his clothes not be burned?" Proverbs 6:27.

PRAYERS TO SEEK DIVINE DIRECTION FOR YOUR MARRIAGE

1. O Lord, give me your divine blueprint for my marriage.
2. Lord, after the order of Joseph, please speak to me in a language that I can understand.
3. O Lord, by your mercy reveal your mind to me on this issue of marriage.
4. Holy Spirit, disorganize my life and reorganize it to fulfill my marital destiny.
5. O Lord, help me to discover my divine purpose in marriage.
6. O Lord, enable me to fulfill my divine purpose in marriage.
7. O Lord, anoint me to locate my God ordained spouse.
8. Spiritual blindness, my life is not your candidate. Therefore die now.
9. Spiritual deafness, my life is not your candidate. Therefore die now.
10. O Lord, please make your way plain before me on this issue of marriage and remove any confusion.
11. Every power manipulating my dreams and imagination to confuse me, die.
12. Spirit of error and mistake, my life is not your candidate, therefore die.
13. O Lord, if I am on the wrong track, correct me, in Jesus name.
14. Lord, plant me by Your traffic light, to know when to wait, get ready, and get going.
15. You my marital destiny refuse to be satanically diverted.
16. Every power saying no to God's yes for my life in marriage, somersault and die.

3. KNOW THE SECRETS

There are certain information that will help us to make godly choices and decisions about marriage that are hidden beneath the surface. These are not obvious so we have to dig below the surface to unearth them. To jump into a relationship without unearthing them is an invitation to a problematic marriage. We should use both spiritual and physical means to find out such information. In doing this, we have to remember that God holds all the secrets that we need to prosper in every area of our life, including marriage.

"The secret things belong unto the LORD our God: but those things which are revealed belong unto us and to our children for ever, that we may do all the words of this law." Deuteronomy 29:29.

It is our job to find out such secrets. **Proverbs 25:2.** The Bible stresses the need for us to get and apply divine wisdom in conducting our lives. **Proverbs 4:7.** It also says that a house is built by wisdom and established by understanding. **Proverbs 24:3.** Therefore, we need both wisdom and understanding to secure a divinely approved and great marriage. Jesus is the wisdom of God and so He is the source of all wisdom and we can access all wisdom through Him. **1 Corinthians 1:24.** The Bible encourages anyone that lacks wisdom to ask God for it.

"If any of you lack wisdom, let him ask of God, that giveth to all men liberally, and upbraideth not; and it shall be given him." James 1:5.

Therefore, we have to through prayers find out divine beneficial secrets that will enable us to do it right in marriage this time around. This is even more so if we failed in a previous marriage or marital relationship. Wisdom demands that we first identify and deal with what caused problems for us in previous relationships before venturing into another one. It is important that we do so because if we do things the same way as before, we will end up with the same result as before which is failure, tears, sorrow, regret, lack of fulfillment, separation, and divorce.

Therefore, we should pray targeted prayers and go through counseling and deliverance if necessary to find out why certain issues keep coming up in our marital lives. These issues include constant rejection, disappointment, delays, and attraction to wrong people. Prayers, counseling, and deliverance, when done properly, can put divine revelation and information at our disposal that will move our marital lives forward. Scriptures confirm this:

"It is the glory of God to conceal a matter; to search out a matter is the glory of kings." Proverbs 25:2.

As Christians, it is our covenant right as God's children to go to Him directly and obtain information that we need to live godly lives and to do it right in every area of our lives, including marriage.

"Call unto me, and I will answer thee, and show thee great and mighty things, which thou knowest not." Jeremiah 33:3.

We do not have to rely on others to seek the Lord for us concerning our marriage. If we go to Him directly and ask Him, He will show us our secret enemies and the secret battles that are raging against our getting married. We can then ask Him to help us crush these battles.

In my case, I had several dreams of being rejected by men. On inquiry, the Lord told me that the problem originated from my foundation. The problem, He said, was further compounded by a former suitor who for his own diabolical reasons put a spell on me to repel prospective suitors and drive them away. I went for deliverance and was set free. Thank God for the ministry of deliverance. God is mighty to deliver. Somebody Him the praise.

In another case, the Lord revealed to a sister after special prayers that it was her name that was keeping prospective suitors away and preventing her from getting married. The meaning of her name was "I am the property of "Ifa"." "Ifa" is an African idol that is worshiped in Africa and other parts of the world. All the members of her family bore the same evil name and were all dedicated to "Ifa." Spiritually, you are married to any power that you are dedicated to. **Numbers 25:3-5.**

In effect, through the evil dedication, they were all married to Ifa and owned by him. The spiritual realm supersedes the physical so as long as she remained married to Ifa in the spirit realm, there could be no marriage for her in the physical The way out for her was for her to change her name and then go through deliverance to verbally renounce, revoke, and break the evil covenants and soul ties keeping the evil marriage in place.

Are you in that situation today? Did your parents covenant and marry you off to some strange power, personality, or idol? Did they collect a spiritual dowry on your head? It is a valid marriage which will not go away on its own unless you properly renounce and separate yourself from it. If you do not do so, it will continue to make your life hell on earth, not only in the area of marriage but in other areas as well such as business, career, and relationships.   It will also affect your children. Please contact a well-trained experienced deliverance minister today. **(See the appendix section for help in doing this).**

Do Your Research Thoroughly

In finding out secrets about your prospective partner, you should ask questions and find out information about your proposed spouse now rather than later when it is too late because marriage is a lifetime commitment. As mentioned above, spiritually you should ask God pertinent questions. Physically, you should also do your research and ask questions from the right sources. Below are some of the questions that you should ask. Please note that these questions apply to both men and women. Also, they are guidelines so you can add other questions as well.

You should ask questions about his spirituality. Is the person genuinely born again or just pretending? How involved is he with the work of God? What is his relationship with his church leadership? Does he have a good reputation in his church and in the larger community? Will he support your calling and ministry? For example, will he let you go on retreats to seek God without being suspicious or abusive? Is he interested in growing spiritually like you or is he satisfied staying in one spot for years? Are you a Holy of Holies Christian while he is content remaining in the Outer Court with no interest in seeking the deep things of God?

You should ask questions about his health. Is the person sickly? Does he require special physical care? If he does, can you handle it and live with it for the rest of your life? For example, does he need daily insulin shots, blood transfusions, dialysis, or periodic hospitalization? Is he epileptic? Does he have special dietary needs? Does he have sickle cell anemia?

What are his or her values? The Bible clearly says that two people can only work together if they are in agreement. **Amos 3:3.** Are you on the same page on major issues of life such as premarital sex and cohabitation; homosexuality; where to live; how to raise the children; money and finance; the role of sex in a marriage; and where to worship after the marriage?

Examine His Spiritual and Physical Background

In finding out the beneficial secrets, there should be a thorough examination of the spiritual and physical background of your proposed spouse. Are there spiritual problems? Are there family idols that need to be destroyed? Is there witchcraft in his the blood line? Are they involved in marine worship? Do his people belong to occult groups such as Freemason, Rosicrucian, AMORC, Lodge, Grail Message, and various new age groups? Are they in demonic cults? Are there collective captivity problems in the family or in their place of birth or origin? These include terminal sicknesses like cancer; tragedies; suicide; drunkenness; addictions; insanity; broken or unstable marriages; and untimely death. Are there evil patterns such as sickle cell anemia, epilepsy, seizures, insanity, sexual looseness or perversion, polygamy, divorce, and teen pregnancy?

This exercise should be taken very seriously and thoroughly carried out. As the scripture below implies, when you marry him, you and your children will acquire these traits so you should address them first before committing to any marital relationship.

"What? know ye not that he which is joined to an harlot is one body? for two, saith he, shall be one flesh." 1 Corinthians 6:16.

How will you fit into his/her larger family?

In examining the spiritual and physical background you should also find out how you will fit into his larger family. This is because no man is an island. Moreover, in most cultures in the world when you marry into a family you de facto marry the entire family. You should inquire about this through prayers before venturing into the relationship. A good question to ask the Lord is, "Will his family accept me?"

You should also prayerfully inquire about the spiritual and physical state of the children. Are there children from previous relationships, particularly young children? If so, how do you plan to win their love and trust? You should have a plan for incorporating them into the relationship and household. You should also consider the financial burden of raising these children. Are you ready to pay the price of sacrificing your comfort and your time to help raise them? Are you ready to love the children unconditionally? Will you still love them even if your love and efforts are neither appreciated nor reciprocated?

Are these children born again? Do they love Jesus? Do they have special callings and gifting on their lives that will need to be developed? What will be the cost, financial and otherwise, of developing these? Are they demonized or bewitched and need deliverance? Are they into drug addiction, witchcraft or the occult? Have they been abused and need extra love and care? Are there physical, spiritual, or emotional handicaps that need to be accommodated?

You should also consider other miscellaneous circumstances surrounding your prospective marital relationship. If you are from different tribes or countries you should consider how this will impact the relationship. What about language and other cultural differences? If you both own your own home, what will happen after the marriage? Will you need to sell one of the houses? If so, whose?

In summary, all these issues mentioned above and other miscellaneous issues that may come up later should be discussed and sorted out before marriage. You should be in agreement because the Bible says that two people can only walk together when they are agreement. **Amos 3:3.**

Please note that the presence of these issues does not necessarily mean that the Lord has not ordained both of you to get married. It simply means that getting married is a process and that a part of that process is to resolve all potentially troublesome issues before the actual marriage takes place. This is to prevent too much stress from being put on the marriage later. Scriptures also counsel on the need for planning and preparation before going into any new venture particularly major ones such as marriage:

"For which of you, intending to build a tower, sitteth not down first, and counteth the cost, whether he have sufficient to finish it lest haply, after he hath laid the foundation and is not able to finish it, all that behold it begin to mock him, saying This man began to build, and was not able to finish?" Luke 14:28-30.

Divine wisdom, therefore, cannot be over emphasized in this area. Even after the initial finding out of the secrets that can affect the relationship, we still have to walk in wisdom continuously throughout the relationship, including during courtship and marriage. All prospective marital partners should be presented to God through prayers for screening and approval before proceeding any further.

We should let God show us when and where to cast our marital nets in the ocean of life. This will ensure that we catch good fish and not just any fish or even rotten fish. The very fish that belongs to you will locate you by fire this season in the mighty name of Jesus. Amen!!! Receive your right match in marriage in Jesus name.

DO IT RIGHT THIS TIME

PRAYERS TO KNOW DIVINE SECRETS

1. O Lord, show me the hidden veiled things concerning this relationship, in the mighty name of Jesus.

2. Holy Spirit divine, all revelation flows from you. Reveal to me all that I need to know about this person (mention his or her name in full) and this relationship, whether good or bad, in the name of Jesus.

3. O Lord, show me your beneficial secrets for my life and marriage in the name of Jesus.

4. O Lord, guide me into the mysteries of my marital life in the name of Jesus.

5. O Lord, visit me and reveal to me secrets that I need to know that will move my marital destiny forward.

6. Every secret covenant, curse, judgment, and vow affecting my marital destiny negatively, break and be canceled by the blood of Jesus.

7. Every ancestral secret hindering my marital progress, be revealed, in the name of Jesus.

8. Evil secret activities currently affecting my life and marriage, be exposed and disgraced, in the name of Jesus.

9. Every power that wants my efforts to turn against me, I pull you down, in the name of Jesus.

10. O Lord, call forth new patterns in my life that will promote my marital destiny, in the name of Jesus.

11. Wicked elders working against my marital well-being, be exposed and disgraced, in the name of Jesus.

12. Wicked elders obstructing me at the gate of my marital breakthrough fall down and die.

13. Blood of Jesus, thunder of God open up all good gates shut against me and my marriage.

14. O God, rebuild the damaged walls of my marital destiny.

15. Every completed work of darkness concerning my marital destiny and my life, be cancelled and let the effect go back to the sender in Jesus name.

29

4. THE RELATIONSHIP SHOULD ALIGN WITH GOD'S WORD

The word of God must be present in any godly marriage. In deciding whether to enter a marital relationship with any person, the rules laid down in the word of God regarding courtship and marriage should be strictly adhered to. These rules include not going into a relationship with an unbeliever; married people; people of the same sex; and close family members. There are other types of relationships that are also expressly forbidden or discouraged in the Bible. They can be found in **2 Corinthians 6:14-16 and Leviticus 20.**

5. WATCH AND PRAY YOUR WAY THROUGH

The Bible tells us that if we abide in Christ and His word abides in us then we can ask anything of the Father and He will give it to us. **John 15:7; 16.** Also the scripture below promises us that when we ask God for a spouse, He will not give us a bad one but give us the very best that there is:

"Ask, and it shall be given you; seek, and ye shall find; knock, and it shall be opened unto you: For everyone that asketh receiveth; and he that seeketh findeth; and to him that knocketh it shall be opened. Or what man is there of you, whom if his son ask bread, will he give him a stone? Or if he ask a fish, will he give him a serpent? If ye then, being evil, know how to give good gifts unto your children, *how much more shall your Father which is in heaven give good things to them that ask him?"* **Matthew 7:7-11.**

The Bible tells us that it is only the correct kind of prayers that will yield the desired answers. **James 5:16.** It also tells us that it is possible to pray and not get the desired result because you went about it the wrong way:

"Ye lust, and have not: ye kill and desire to have, and cannot obtain: ye fight and war, yet ye have not, because ye ask not. *Ye ask, and* *receive not, because ye ask amiss, that ye may consume it upon your lusts."* James 4:2-3.

Praying the wrong way could mean praying wrong prayers; praying the correct prayer at the wrong time; or not praying a particular prayer long enough for it to have an impact. For example, if household witchcraft powers are delaying your marriage, you should pray against them between 12 midnight and 3 a.m., which is when witches typically hold their meetings. You also have to bombard them with fast, furious and sustained prayers, to force them to leave you alone because they are stubborn. This will require you to pray every day at mid night for twenty one days of more. You should endeavor not to miss any days so that you do not give the enemy the opportunity to reinforce against you. This ensures that there is constant bombardment which gives the enemy no time to regroup, reinforce, or counter attack making victory easier.

Therefore, you should go beyond just praying general prayers for marriage. You should also engage in prayers that are targeted at resolving specific problems that you are encountering in this area of your life. They should be prayers that have been proven to work for the particular problems which may be household witchcraft, cobwebs, marine witchcraft, envious witchcraft, evil dedication, spiritual marriage, rejection, and others.

This will require discipline on your part. For example, you may have to stay up at night to pray or have to pray a particular prayer over an extended period. But always remember no pain, no gain. Remember also that this time around, we are doing it differently. We are doing it right this time around. Be encouraged. As you do, God will visit you and change your marital story.

There are various issues to pray about in the area of marriage. First, you should pray to repair your foundation because a faulty foundation cannot carry a good marriage. Pray to know the secrets behind any existing marital problems such as why there are no suitors; why you experience constant disappointment and rejection in courtship; why you are attracted to wrong people, and why your previous marriage or marital relationship failed. You should pray to know whom God has ordained for you in marriage and not just pick anybody. Pray against the spirit of

31

error and mistake. Pray against powers magnetizing the wrong people to you. Pray also against powers that are assigned to satanically divert you to wrong relationships that God has not ordained for you. This is to ensure that you pick the wrong spouse, end up in a bad marriage, and fail to fulfill your destiny. Pray that the Lord will reveal to you beneficial secrets that will help you make the right decisions and choices this time around. Pray for divine favor each step of the way and that like Queen Esther you will be the Hadassah, the divinely favored and chosen one of your God ordained spouse. **Esther 2:17-18.** Pray against untimely death before and during the marriage.

Pray against bewitchment of your marital destiny. Witchcraft and ancestral powers manipulate people into wrong marriages to truncate their glorious destinies. So you have to set their monitoring gadgets on fire. You should use prayers to separate yourself from every evil tree that is representing you or harboring your wedding garment, shoes, and rings and then set it on fire.

Pray that every evil cage holding your spouse should break and release him or her. Pray that he or she be released from every spell and command every evil bus stop where he has wrongly packed the vehicle of his marital destiny out of bewitchment to eject him. Then set the evil bus stop on fire. So long as your partner is tied down in the wrong place and tied up in the wrong relationship he or she cannot be available for you. Command every evil rope tying your partner up and making him or her unavailable for you to catch fire. Remember to pray these same prayers for yourself also.

All stubborn spirit spouses must be castrated, divorced, and set ablaze. You should also set on fire the evil wedding ring put on your finger by the spirit spouse as this affirms the evil marriage; reinforces his ownership claim over your life; and prevents the real God ordained marriage from manifesting. All these are done through praying targeted prayers.

Pray for the eyes and ears of your God ordained spouse to be open to the Holy Spirit's leading. It is one thing for God to show you your divine partner, it is another thing entirely for that person to see and accept you as his or her partner. The Lord compares a person that kick's against

God's given instructions and direction to an ignorant mule that lacks understanding:

"I will instruct you and teach you in the way which you should go: I will guide you with my eyes. Be ye not as the horse, or as the mule, which have no understanding: whose mouth must be held in with bit and bridle, lest they come near unto thee." Psalm 32:8-9.

Pray that every barrier, satanic embargo, and wall of partition, separating you from your spouse should collapse after the order of the wall of Jericho. Pray that he or she will be able to see beyond these satanically inspired walls that make you seem incompatible and see that God created you to complement and bring out the best in each other.

Pray to be at the right place at the right time. If you are in London and your spouse is in Japan, it will be very difficult to meet. You should also pray against satanic delay, slow and sluggish progress, and lateness in goodness in marriage. Ask the Lord to hasten things. **Jeremiah 1:12.**

Pray the prayers at the end of the section "know the secret" often, to invite the Holy Spirit into your situation and inquire from Him new developments that you need to pray about concerning your marital journey. Pray in the Holy Ghost often because the Holy Spirit intercedes for us, particularly when we do not know what to pray. **Romans 8:26.**

The Bible tells us to watch and prayer so you should not only pray but watch also. **Colossian 4:2.** Take time periodically to seat before the Lord to watch and pray. You can set aside some weekends for this. You should take note of your dreams and revelations and write them down. They will aid you in your fasting and prayers. They will also help you in making good decisions later. For example, if the Holy Spirit has already identified your spouse, it is pointless to continue to pray the prayers on knowing the will of God. If you are dreaming of you and your partner always having your back turned to each other, then you have to pray against demonic walls and barriers separating you. Until you do that God is unlikely to show you anymore new things to pray about.

If you do not understand what God is saying to you through your dreams then ask Him. If you are still not sure then seek godly counsel.

In summary, you should pray for success in the various stages of the marital process. This should include prayers to determine God's will; to locate your partner; to remove barriers; for a godly courtship; favor with your partner and prospective in laws; and for the success of the courtship and various marriage ceremonies including the court and church.

Even now, it is not too early to start praying concerning child bearing and rearing. As you buy things for your wedding by faith, you can also include things for the baby as a prophetic action to back up your faith that the marriage will be fruitful.

As you pray these prayers, I pray that God will visit you and elevate you matrimonially. I prophesy that this year people will join you to celebrate your wedding in the name of Jesus. This year you shall be celebrated in the name of Jesus. Pray like this:

Every power programmed to disgrace me on my day of glory, somersault and die now, in the name of Jesus.

PRAYERS FOR MARITAL BREAKTHOUGH

1. Every power, spirit, and personality manipulating my life, fall down and die in the name of Jesus.

2. Every power, spirit, and personality manipulating my God ordained partner's life, fall down and die in the name of Jesus.

3. Blood of Jesus, deliver me from every satanic manipulation aimed at changing my marital destiny.

4. O Lord, help my God ordained spouse to look beyond the barriers separating us and to see me and accept me as his/her own.

5. Every wall of Jericho separating me from my God ordained spouse, crumble, in the name of Jesus.

6. Blood of Jesus, deliver me from the effect of every step that I have taken that will lead me to marital destruction.

7. O Lord, deliver me from the effect of wrong choices made in the past that are bringing affliction into my life now.

8. Spirit of error and mistake I am not your candidate, therefore, die.

9. Direct me, O Lord, whenever I am threatened by error and mistake, in the name of Jesus.

10. Misleading demons leading me into wrong relationships release me and die.

11. Every seed and root of nakedness in my foundation, wither and die.

12. My Lord and My God let your glory cover my nakedness today.

13. Blood of Jesus, fire of the Holy Ghost, restore the communication line between me and my God ordained partner, that witchcraft powers have stolen.

14. Every satanic broadcaster assigned against my marital progress, die.

15. Every evil magnet attracting the wrong partners to me, scatter by fire.

16. Powers aborting my marital breakthroughs at the edge of success die.

17. Monitoring powers assigned against my marital breakthroughs, be buried.

18. Evil eyes monitoring my marriage go blind by fire.

19. Evil horns scattering my marital breakthrough, be cut off.

22. I prophesy breakthroughs into every area of my life. (Name them.)

6. PLUG INTO A HOLY GHOST CENTERED CHURCH

God does not want us to forsake the company of other saints. **Hebrews 10:25.** A lone ranger is easy prey for the devil, the roaring lion that is looking for who to devour and his well-trained agents. Moreover, if you do not keep the company of God's people you will end up in the company of enemy. I pray that you will not marry your enemy.

God should be involved in the search for a home church. Ask Him to lead you to His church for you. You can adapt the prayer points on divine direction and knowing divine secrets above to help you in doing this. Look for a church where the fullness of the Holy Ghost and the power of God dwell. They should believe in the totality of the word of God including salvation, healing, deliverance, and spiritual warfare. Look for one where yokes are broken off lives; the oppressed and bound are set free; and lives are changed. Please stay away from all those worldly, entertainment, and dating services that they have in some churches under the guise of "singles group." All sorts of immorality are allowed to fester in some of these groups in a bid to be "current". The word of God has never changed and will never change. This is because it is forever settled in heaven and on earth. The standard of God remains the same. He has never and will not condone fornication and immorality, particularly in the house of God.

You should seek out instead, a church where there is godly leadership and oversight. It should be one where the singles meet often to pray; fast; search the word together; do spiritual warfare; encourage one another; fellowship; and periodically go through deliverance.

7. PATIENCE AND PERSEVERANCE

God is very time conscious and works by times and seasons. As far as He is concerned, there is a divine time and a season appointed for everything under the sun. **Ecclesiastes 3:1.** Every vision that originates from God, including the one for your marriage, is for an appointed time.

"For the vision is yet for an appointed time, but at the end it shall speak, and not lie: though it tarry, wait for it; because it will surely come, it will not tarry." Habakkuk 2:3.

"Is anything too hard for the Lord? At the time appointed, I will return unto thee, according to the time of life, and Sarah shall have a son." Genesis 18:14.

The period between when God gives us a promise for our lives and when the promise actually comes to pass is usually a very difficult time. It requires patience and perseverance on our part. It is also a delicate time because what we do or fail to do during this period can facilitate or abort our breakthroughs.

So what should we do during this period while waiting for God's promises to come to pass in our lives? We should nurture God's promises to us with prayers; fasting; and confessing and standing on the word of God that relates to the promises until the appointed time for its fulfillment comes.

To receive the fullness of your matrimonial breakthrough and not just a portion, you have to be patient and endure. If you do not do this you may end up with an Ishmael. An Ishmael is something that is good but not God's best for you. It is a thorn in the flesh.

The Bible says better is the end of a thing than the beginning thereof. **Ecclesiastes 7:8**. Therefore, we should emulate Abraham who overcame through patience and endurance and saw God's promise of a son fulfilled after twenty five years of waiting and trusting God.

"And so, after he had patiently endured, he obtained the promise." Hebrews 6:15.

On the other hands, we should also learn from the mistakes of Abraham's, who in a bid to help God, ran ahead of God's timing and ended up giving birth to Ishmael who has been a thorn in his flesh ever since. Therefore, as you wait for that appointed time, you should be patient; set your face like flint; and continuously say to yourself like Job:

"All the days of my appointed time will I wait, till my change come." Job 14:14.

You should also realize that sometimes God allows "Saul" to come first. Then he invariably messes up, paving the way for your "David," God's genuinely choice for you in marriage to show up.

Arrogance and pride may have made Saul feel that he could not obey God and accept you as God's choice for him in marriage. **Psalm 32:8-9**. He may even have heard God clearly but chose to disobey His instructions because he wanted to do his own thing. The agenda of the Almighty was not as important to him as his own agenda and the opinion of men. **John 12:43**. He had his idol and wanted to fulfill the lust of his eyes, his heart, and his flesh.

Saul chose not to enter the Holy of Holies, the place of the perfect will of God, preferring instead to remain in the Outer Court, the place of the permissive will of God. He created his own "Ishmael" and then presented it to God to bless. Then he turned around and said to you, "God has not told me that you are my divine partner." Please do not take this personally. Realize that it is not you that he has rejected but God and His choice for him in marriage. Remember what the Lord said to the Prophet Samuel concerning King Saul. He said that it was not the Prophet Samuel that Saul had rejected but the God whom Samuel represented. **1 Samuel 8:7.**

Remember also that even Jesus, the Son of God, was rejected. But did He not still fulfill His divine destiny? Yes, He did! You too will fulfill your divine marital destiny in Jesus name. God will heal every hurt and every emotional scar left in your life by rejection. The sun will shine again. There will yet be joy in the morning for you in marriage. This is your season of Joy in Jesus name. I say your Sunday, your season of marital rest and fulfilment, is here, in Jesus name. This year you shall join the company of the married in Jesus name.

Leave Saul alone! Wipe your tears! It was never meant to be. If he had been yours, none would have been able to take him away. God will reward your obedience to Him and your labor of love squandered on "Saul." He has tested you and found you faithful. He will compensate you for that by giving you the very best spouse there is in Jesus name. No power, no personality, or spirit can stop you now.

If "Saul" does not go then your "David", the man or woman after God's own heart that God has prepared for you, will never show up. Beloved please wipe your tears. Let go, and let God. Stop crying over "Saul". The Lord is saying to you today, like He said to the Prophet Samuel, to let go and move on for your "David" awaits you. **1 Samuel 16:1**

Moreover, you can be sure that if "Saul" refused to listen to God's voice in the area of marriage, he will also refuse to listen to God in other critical issues of life later in the marriage. Such a marriage would be tantamount to going on a high speed race with a drunk driver on the steering wheel. The vehicle will certainly capsize down the road with you in it. So let him go! Stop crying! Again, the Lord is saying to you today that He has a "David" prepared and waiting to replace "Saul" in your life. **1 Samuel 16:1.** He will reveal him to you in due time in Jesus name.

Please sing this chorus with me as we encourage ourselves in the Lord:

> I will wait patiently for the Lord
> I will wait patiently for the Lord
> The Lord is my shepherd
> I will wait patiently for the Lord
> The Lord is my shepherd
> I will wait patiently for the Lord

To further encourage yourself in the Lord, please meditate on the following scriptures. They will encourage you as you wait patiently for God and His timing for your wonderful marriage:

"I had fainted, unless I had believed to see the goodness of the LORD in the land of the living. Wait on the LORD: be of good courage, and he shall strengthen thine heart: wait, I say, on the LORD." Psalm 27:13-14.

"I waited patiently for the LORD; and he inclined unto me, and heard my cry." Psalm 40:1.

"Rest in the LORD, and wait patiently for him." Psalm 37:7.

"Better is the end of a thing than the beginning thereof: and the patient in spirit is better than the proud in spirit." Ecclesiastes 7:8.

END OF CHAPTER PRAYERS

1. Father, pour upon me today the grace to wait on you patiently for my marriage.

2. Every power blocking my marital harvest, die now.

3. Every evil tongue pronouncing curses on my marital blessings, receive your curses back on your head, in the name of Jesus.

4. Every evil hand militating against God's best for me in marriage, be cut off by the sword of God, in the name of Jesus.

5. By fire, by force, I strip off every garment of reproach and I put on the garment of a better marriage in the name of Jesus.

6. All my accumulated breakthroughs, including marriage, manifest in my life by fire.

7. Every power of the night sitting on my glorious things in marriage, be unseated and die.

8. Every animal programmed into my life to slow down my marital progress, die.

9. Any witchcraft broom sweeping away good things from my life and marriage, catch fire and burn to ashes.

10. Every evil cauldron manipulating my life and marriage, be smashed to irreparable pieces.

11. Every power behind marital problems in my life, I bury you now.

12. Power of restoration fall upon every department of my life now.

CHAPTER 5

SEVEN INGREDIENTS OF A GOOD MARRIAGE

The foundation for a good marriage is laid a long time before the couple actually exchange marriage vows in church. The seven ingredients of a good marriage are guidelines set forth in the word of God to guide us in entering a godly marriage. Following them will result in a fulfilling and enduring union and not just another marriage to be endured like so many out there today.

Getting married the God prescribed way so as to produce the God ordained marriage is a process. The output of any process is only as good as the inputs. I have used the title "Ingredients of a good marriage," for this chapter because the process of bringing a godly marriage into being is similar to that of cooking a pot of soup. To end up with a nutritious and delicious pot of soup you have to use good quality and correct ingredients. You also have to follow the steps specified in the recipe as to what, how, and when to use the various ingredients in the preparation of the soup.

The process of getting married is the same. The institution of marriage like everything else that God created has a divine purpose. This means that God had a glorious picture in His mind of what marriage should be when He created it. For the marriage process to end up in the wonderful marriage of God's vision certain ingredients have to be put into the relationship right from the beginning. Certain steps also have to be followed in birthing the marriage. God has His own calendar for this process and each step of the process has a divine time element attached to it. **Ecclesiastes 3:1.**

41

The process will not end in the wonderful marriage that God envisioned if you omit key ingredients; use low quality or wrong ingredients; or fail to follow the steps specified in the recipe in preparing the soup. Assuming you decide to cook a pot of soup but because you are in hurry to eat it, the sand was not washed off the vegetables or the fish deboned. The meat was put in last when it should have been put in first to have enough time to cook. Oil and to add salt were not added for taste and instead of pepper, a required ingredient, you put soy sauce.

The bottom line is that you ended up with an unpalatable and undesirable product because you omitted key ingredients in the recipe; used wrong ingredients; or failed to clean or prepare them properly. You also did not follow the steps stipulated on the recipe for cooking the soup or you reordered them. It was a wasted effort and you labored in vain because even though you took a shorter time and less work to prepare the soup, no one can eat it as it has no taste; the meat is uncooked; and it is full of bones and sand. Your hope was dashed as your vision of eating good soup at the end of your efforts did not materialize.

Actualizing a godly marriage is a similar process to the one described above for preparing a good pot of soup. Certain ingredients have to be present in a relationship for a godly and fulfilling marriage to emerge from the process. If these ingredients are absent; their quality compromised; or critical steps in the marriage process are skipped; and you rush into marriage; the end result will be an unpalatable marriage. You will be heading for a ship wreck down the road.

We will now take a look at these ingredients that should be present for a good and godly marriage to emerge. But before we do that, let us make the following declarations loud and clear:

1. I will not use my own hands to wreck the vehicle of my marital destiny in Jesus name
2. I will not close the door of marriage against myself in the name of Jesus.
3. On this issue of marriage, I refuse to cooperate with the enemy.

1. HOLY AND GODLY COURTSHIP

A holy courtship is very important simply because an unholy courtship can easily degenerate into the sin of fornication and immorality. Fornication is sex outside of marriage. It vandalizes a person's destiny and lays a bad foundation for any marriage. The Bible forbids it and describes it as self-destructive as you actually sin against your own self when you engage in it. Its effect is so devastating that the Bible commands us to flee from it:

"*Flee fornication. Every sin that a man doeth is without the body; but he that committeth fornication sinneth against his own body. What?* know ye not that your body is the temple of the Holy Ghost which is in you, which ye have of God, and ye are not your own? For ye are bought with a price: therefore glorify God in your body, and in your spirit, which are God's." 1 Corinthians 6:18-20.

The Christian courtship process is quite different from the worldly dating process used by the unbelievers around us. It requires that you first ask God through prayers to give you His ordained spouse for you. Then you patiently wait on Him until He does. You do not run ahead of Him by picking a spouse for yourself no matter how tempting, available, or suitable they may appear to be.

The Christian courtship process does not allow you to pick a spouse for yourself and then ask God after doing so to rubber stamp him or her for you. Instead you should first ask God for a spouse and then patiently allow Him to pick one for you. This is the Bible way as we can see in the process that was used to get a wife for Isaac, Abraham's son in the Bible. **Genesis 24:1-67.**

The Christian courtship process does not allow the sampling of various members of the opposite sex in the name of "dating." This will only scar the emotions, put evil soul ties in place, and mar the prospect of having a healthy and fulfilling marriage later. This is particularly true where sex is involved.

You should first take the time in fasting and prayers to find out from God who your right marital partner is before courtship can even start. A person may be available but not be God's choice for you. Keep in mind that not every man is your husband and not every woman is your wife. Therefore, you should take everyone that approaches you for marriage to God in prayer. There is no short cut. You should pray and fast for at least three days. Even if you believe that God has spoken to you on the first day, you should still pray for at least two more days to confirm what you believe God has told you. You can even ask Him to confirm it through independent sources.

If you believe that God has shown you His ordained partner for your life, you should notify the people that have spiritual oversight over you. This will be discussed more extensively under the section "Seek Godly Counsel."

There should be no sex before or during courtship. You have to wait until after the marriage. There should also be abstinence from all sorts of sexual perversion, such as oral sex, anal sex, pornography, playing with sex toys, or whatever sexual deviance is out there in the world today.

There should be no fondling, kissing, and all other defiling actions that open the door for bondages and demonic oppression such as pollution and harassment by spirit spouses. Moreover, these actions incurs God's wrath and can abort destinies as the scripture below says:

"But fornication, and all uncleanness, or covetousness, let it not be once named among you, as becometh saints; Neither filthiness, nor foolish talking, nor jesting, which are not convenient: but rather giving of thanks. For this ye know, that no whoremonger, nor unclean person, nor covetous man, who is an idolater, hath any inheritance in the kingdom of Christ and of God. Let no man deceive you with vain words: for because of these things cometh the wrath of God upon the children of disobedience." Ephesians 5:1-6.

You have to tread with care in this area, by avoiding situations, people, and places that can make you to compromise and bring reproach to Christ, His church, and yourself. The Bible warns us in **Proverbs 6:27:**

"Can a man take fire in his bosom and not be burned?"

It goes further to show us the danger that such rash actions pose to our lives:

"He that diggeth a pit shall fall into it; and whoso breaketh an hedge, a serpent shall bite him." Ecclesiastes 10:8.

The Bible counsels that the key to avoiding these various pitfalls and sins is to daily hide the word of God in our hearts. **Psalm 119:9.** Isaac was meditating on the word of God when his wife, Rebecca, was brought to him. **Genesis 24:63.** Can the same be said of you today? Are you allowing evil thoughts to take over your life? Remember that fornication and adultery are sins that can be committed in the heart as well as through the actual physical act.

"But I say unto you, that whosever looketh on a woman to lust after her hath committed adultery with her already in his heart." Matthew 5:28.

The Bible cautions us to guard our hearts with all diligence so that they are not defiled. This is important because out of them flow the issues of life and death. **Proverb 4:23.** Therefore, we should consciously censor certain things from getting in there. We are responsible for keeping our thoughts pure:

"Finally, brethren, whatsoever things are true, whatsoever things are honest, whatsoever things are just, whatsoever things are pure, whatsoever thing are lovely, whatsoever things are of good report; if there be any virtue, and if there be any praise, think on these things." Philippians 4:8.

Discipline is required in this very sensitive area. The marital bed must not be defiled. **Hebrews 13:4.** Sex outside of marriage lays a wrong foundation which will create problems later. We should not be ignorant of the devices of the devil and allow him to truncate our lives and marital destiny. **2 Corinthians 2:11.**

The Bible counsels us to get married if we cannot control our emotions and our flesh. **1 Corinthians 7:9.** However, in doing this, God's laid down principles, process, and timing should be followed. We should engage in sex only after the actual solemnization of the marriage in a spirit filled church. These checks and balances are put there for our own good. They are to protect us from bad or broken marriages and all the devastation that comes with it.

Always remember that marital bliss is possible today. Remember also, that you get what you sow. If you put garbage into the marriage process, you will get garbage out of it and not bliss. **Galatians 6:7.** Therefore, it is certain that if you sow thorns you will get thorns. Thorns pricks and it hurts.

2. GENUINE LOVE

"Many waters cannot quench love, neither can the floods drown it: if a man would give all the substance of his house for love, it would utterly be contemned." Song of Solomon 8:6-7.

"So ought men to love their wives as their own bodies. He that loveth his wife loveth himself." Ephesians 5:28.

In the scripture above we are told that many waters cannot quench genuine love. The Bible also teaches us that love is better than life. **Psalm 63:3.** Love also we are told covers a multitude of sins. **1 Peter 4:7-9; Proverbs 10:12.** This quality of love to cover a multitude of sins is very important because marriage is a life time commitment.

The kind of love that should be evident in a godly marital relationship is the agape type of love. All other kinds of love, such as erotic love, can come later in the relationship. Agape love is not selfish or self-centered but puts the other person first. It should be selfless like the love between our Lord Jesus and His Church that prompted Him to die for it. It is committed to making the relationship work. This kind of love is described in great details in **1 Corinthians chapter 13** below:

"If I speak in the tongues of men or of angels, but do not have love, I am only a resounding gong or a clanging cymbal. If I have the gift of prophecy and can fathom all mysteries and all knowledge, and if I have a faith that can move mountains, but do not have love, I am nothing. If I give all I possess to the poor and give over my body to hardship that I may boast, but do not have love, I gain nothing. Love is patient, love is kind. It does not envy, it does not boast, it is not proud. It does not dishonor others, it is not self-seeking, it is not easily angered, it keeps no record of wrongs. Love does not delight in evil but rejoices with the truth. It always protects, always trusts, always hopes, always perseveres. Love never fails. But where there are prophecies, they will cease; where there are tongues, they will be stilled; where there is knowledge, it will pass away. For we know in part and we prophesy in part, but when completeness comes, what is in part disappears. When I was a child, I talked like a child, I thought like a child, I reasoned like a child. When I became a man, I put the ways of childhood behind me. For now we see only a reflection as in a mirror; then we shall see face to face. Now I know in part; then I shall know fully, even as I am fully known. And now these three remain: faith, hope and love. But the greatest of these is love."

If we really want to do it right this time, we should meditate often on **1 Corinthians 13** and digest it because it tells us how a loving relationship should function. It also gives us some of the vital ingredients that are necessary for building a stable marital relationship and home. These include patience, kindness, and forgiveness.

God is love. **1 John 4:7-8.** Love, therefore, constitutes is a good foundation on which to build a godly marriage. Infatuation and lust on the other hand are not because they originate from the flesh and are capricious. Such a marriage will not stand the test of time. We should learn from the mistakes of Samson who allowed lust, infatuation, indiscipline, and his flesh to truncate his glorious destiny by marrying an unbeliever. **Judges 14:1-7, 16:4**. The result was betrayal, bondage, and untimely death.

3. PICK YOUR FRIENDS CAREFULLY

Who do you associate with? You have to break away from the ungodly people around you. This includes even those who hide in the household of God to do evil. If you do not, they will not only pollute you but they will lure you into joining them to do evil and offending God. The Bible counsels us that:

"Evil communication corrupts good manners." 1 Corinthians 15:33.

It also warns that if you hang out with losers you will become a loser yourself:

"He that walketh with wise men shall be wise: but a companion of fools shall be destroyed." Proverbs 13:20.

If they are not heading in the same direction that God is taking you or if their values conflict with godly values, then they should not be your friends. You should stay away from them because friendship with them can destroy you and your marital destiny as we see in the psalm below:

"Blessed is the man that walketh not in the counsel of the ungodly, nor standeth in the way of sinners, nor sitteth in the seat of the scornful. But his delight is in the law of the LORD; and in his law doth he meditate day and night. And he shall be like a tree planted by the rivers of water, that bringeth forth his fruit in his season; his leaf also shall not wither; and whatsoever he doeth shall prosper. The ungodly are not so: but are like the chaff which the wind driveth away. Therefore the ungodly shall not stand in the judgment, nor sinners in the congregation of the righteous. For the LORD knoweth the way of the righteous: but the way of the ungodly shall perish." Psalm 1:1-6.

4. LET THE MAN DRIVE THE RELATIONSHIP

Sisters listen! Let the men drive the relationship. We should start the relationship as we want it to go on. You should start off on the right note. If you start the relationship off wrongly, it will become a pattern that is carried over into the marriage. The word of God says that the man is the head of the home and the woman is to submit to him. **Ephesians 5:22; Colossians 3:18.** Even if he is younger than you or of a lesser status financially, academically, spiritually, or socially, you should still allow him to take the lead and to be the head that God has called him to be.

What do you see in the special man that God has hand picked out of the whole universe to be your spouse? Do you see him through God's eyes or do you belittle him and compare him to others? Do you build him up or do you tear him down? Do you know what he will become tomorrow? David in the Bible saw himself as a shepherd boy but God saw a king in him and made him one.

The Bible talks about the latter days when men will not be allowed to drive the relationship. Instead, several women, who are desperate to get married, will be pursuing one man. The scripture below describes for us the level of desperation of these women:

"And in that day seven women shall take hold of one man, saying, We will eat our own bread, and wear our own apparel: only let us be called by thy name, to take away our reproach." Isaiah 4:1.

Such marriages would be in name only as the women would offer to do everything that a man should normally be responsible for in the marriage including financial, spiritual, physical, and emotional support.

Today, this spirit is already in the world. There are many gigolos and desperate ladies out there ready to do anything to get married. We should be as wise as serpents in our dealings with such. **Matthew 10:16.** As daughters of Zion, we should be different because our lives should be guided by the rules of the kingdom of God where we are kings. Royal princesses should not cheapen themselves by throwing themselves at men. As a king also, you the brother should not cheapen yourself by accepting or even encouraging such desperate measures from prospective marriage partners. This is because as you make your bed, so you will lie on it. Remember, whatsoever a man tolerates will dominate him.

Please note that I am not advocating that women should be complacent or docile in the area of marriage. You should be an active participant in anything that impacts your life and destiny. After all, Ruth with the help of her mother in law, Naomi, positioned herself very strategically in Boaz's life until he was forced to notice her, take action, and claim her as his wife. **Ruth 3:8-4:12.** I am merely saying that we should let the man "find" the wife as the Bible advocates because there is a special blessing in his doing so:

"Whoever finds a good wife obtains favor of the Lord." Proverbs 18:22.

Allow him to wear the "pants" and drive the relationship. Let him do the pursuing. Marriage should be seen as a once in a lifetime opportunity. So seize the opportunity and enjoy it! Let him spoil you. Sit back, relax, and savor the honor and privilege of being "chased" by your man! This is biblical and it is good for the man and the woman. Enjoy the chase!

A woman should not be so desperate as to beg a man to marry her; manipulate him into a relationship; or even worse still marriage. Not only that, she should not even appear to be doing so. It is a turn off that can make you to lose the man's respect. Let the Holy Spirit have His way instead. If he is not for you, no amount of cajoling, manipulation, and witchcraft prayers can make it work. Many have tried that and they are crying now. Always remember that what God has for you will be yours. Let us tell the devil that through the following song so that he can back off our case. Please sing with me:

What God has for me, it is for me
What God has for me, it is for me
I know without a doubt
That he will bring me out
What God has for me, it is for me

5. AVOID ALL APPEARANCES OF EVIL

The word of God admonishes us to avoid all appearance in our Christian walk with God:

"Abstain from all appearance of evil." 1 Thessalonians 5:22.

This requires us to fear God and out of that fear restrain from doing anything that could hurt His name, His people, and His work. We should not give the unbelievers and baby Christians around us the opportunity to blaspheme the name of the Lord. Rather, we should flee all appearance of evil like Joseph who fled from Potiphar's adulterous wife in such a hurry that he left his jacket behind. **Genesis 39:10-13.**

This is not about actually committing a sin but about avoiding things in a relationship with the opposite sex that people around us can misconstrue and misinterpret. For example, a couple that is intending marriage should not sleep in each other's homes before the marriage takes place. Doing this under any guise will only give the enemy an inroad into the relationship to kill, steal, and destroy. **John 10:10.** This is because emotions can get out of control and before you know it, you have sex, and then end up having a baby out of wedlock. What kind of a witness would you be for Christ then? What kind of a foundation would that create for your marriage?

Never forget that we are the light and the salt of the world. We are God's ambassadors, his witness to those around us. The public only sees and judges what we present to them. Our lives should be the living Bible that they read. Therefore, we should avoid all appearance of evil. Say with me:

"I refuse to bring reproach to my Lord Jesus."

6. SEEK GODLY COUNSEL

"Where no counsel is, the people fall: but in the multitude of counsellors there is safety." Proverbs 11:14.

It is important that you notify church leadership, such as pastors and the marriage committee after you have prayerfully determined who your God ordained partner is. This is for several reasons. The first is that decisions concerning marriage are for life so it is good to get godly counsel before you commit to any relationship. The Bible counsels that there is safety in doing so. **Proverbs 24:6.**

Secondly, it is for the protection of church members, your intended partner, and yourself. It is also to prevent the confusion, mistakes, and deception that is so rampant in the area of marriage. Some brethren for selfish reasons, approach multiple members of a church for marriage claiming to be the partner that God has chosen for them. Some prospective suitors are not even born again while others are satanic agents on assignment for the devil looking for whom to devour. **1 Peter 5:8.** God will help us not to marry our enemies.

Lastly, we should be very careful because as we can see from the following scripture, there is very little room in the Bible for divorce. As far as God is concerned, marriage is a lifelong commitment regardless of whether we are married to the right person or not.

"But I say unto you, that whosoever shall put away his wife, saving for the cause of fornication, causeth her to commit adultery: and whosoever shall marry her that is divorced committed adultery." Matthew 5:32.

You cannot divorce a person because she is too old or is not from your tribe or country. You cannot say after you have had your fill, "It was a business arrangement, I married her to obtain the residency or citizenship of my country of sojourning, so I can divorce her." You cannot even divorce a person because he or she is a witch. As far as God and His word are concerned, "a covenant is a covenant, is a covenant." Therefore, "a marriage is a marriage, is a marriage," a covenant that is

52

binding for life. So it is important to do it right this time around. We will not miss it this time around in the name of Jesus. Amen!!!!

You should seek counsel from those with spiritual oversight over you who are in good standing with God and hear Him clearly. Allow your pastor, youth pastor, or marriage committee, to be involved before you get into the relationship. This is a wise thing to do and has saved many Christians from unnecessary heart aches, pains, and wrecking their destinies.

Some years ago I introduced one of my suitors to my pastor. He asked me, "Where is his wife?" Later, I found out that the man of God was right. The brother had his "Esther," his "favored one," stashed away somewhere for marriage. I was only intended to be his free ticket to the United States.

In another relationship, my pastor gave me a set of prayers to pray. After two weeks of praying against bewitchment, my "prince charming" ran away. Holy Ghost fire pursued him out of my life. What a sweet escape! Praise the Lord! I pray that affliction will not arise a second time in our marital life in the mighty name of Jesus.

The word of God tells us that in the multitude of counselors there is safety. **Proverbs 11:14; Proverbs 24:6.** Therefore, in the heat and infatuation of the moment, even if you think that you are Joseph or Josephina the dreamer, and that God has clearly shown you that a person is your divine partner, you should still seek godly counsel from those that have spiritual oversight over you.

However, even though it is good to seek godly counsel, we should be very careful who we seek such counsel from for several reasons. You could abort a good relationship by seeking counsel from an evil or envious person. You could also seek counsel from pastors who are not grounded in the word of God or that mix Christ with voodoo and other demonic powers. You should also not seek counsel from carnal friends who will advise you without seeking God.

Some people will even encourage you to go into sin and enter fire. They will counsel you that it is okay to have sex since you have agreed to get married. But are you truly getting married? Particularly after the man has had a taste of everything, will he still marry you? Even if he does, the foundation of such a marriage is already defiled. **Hebrews 13:4.**

53

Others, even in the church, will offer to take you to see a "prophet" who is nothing but a glorified diviner, sorcerer, witchdoctor, and voodoo man using the spirit of divination to confuse, manipulate, and divert destinies. You should refuse to go. Some so called "Christians" stoop to using love portions, charms, and witchcraft to hook a spouse.

Brethren, this ought not to be so. When you enter a marriage the wrong way you pay a heavy price later. This is regardless of how rosy it looks at first. Stop and seek godly counsel today about that whirlwind relationship that you are rushing headlong into now. Do it today, before you go in too deep and get burnt in the process. **Proverbs 6:27.**

7. LEAVING AND CLEAVING

"Therefore shall a man leave his father and his mother, and shall cleave unto his wife: and they shall be one flesh." Genesis 2:24.

For both the man and the woman, that want a godly marriage, there should be both a "leaving" of your larger family circle and a "cleaving" to each other. This is so important that not only is it mentioned in the Old Testament, but our Lord Jesus reaffirmed it in the New Testament:

"And said, For this cause shall a man leave father and mother, and shall cleave to his wife: and they twain shall be one flesh?" Matthew 19:5.

In a marital relationship that will succeed, there should be no room for a human third party, not even parents and children. Only God, the brother, and the sister should be involved in the relationship. This forms a three-fold cord that cannot easily be broken. **Ecclesiastes 4:12.**

As a couple, you have to discipline yourself to keep any challenges that you are facing to yourselves. The Bible teaches us the wisdom of keeping our personal business to ourselves. **Micah 7:5.** If there are any problems in the relationship, take them to God in prayers first. If you need further assistance or intervention, go to your pastor, who is God's appointed shepherd over your life. It is best to leave your family members and friends out of it.

54

END OF CHAPTER PRAYERS
My Marriage Appear By Fire

1. Every power behind my going to the market and buying nothing, die, in the name of Jesus.
2. O Lord, in choosing my God ordained spouse, open my eyes to identify every counterfeit and to refuse it, in the name of Jesus.
3. Arrows of confusion and discouragement fired into my marital destiny jump out and backfire.
4. Spirit of mistake and error I bind you, depart from my life.
5. You my "original" God ordained spouse, whoever you are, wherever you are, arise and claim me by fire.
6. Father Lord, correct every negative impression about me in the heart of .... (Put the name of your God ordained spouse.)
7. Every river of bitterness about my life flowing now in the heart of --- dry up. (Put the name of your God ordained spouse.)
8. The name and blood of Jesus shall not fail in my marital situation.
9. Every household power working against my God ordained marriage be disgraced and arrested, in the name of Jesus.
10. I refuse to sit on any evil seat constructed for me by the enemy of my marriage.
11. Every power, spirit, or personality occupying my God ordained marital seat, be unseated by thunder, in the name of Jesus.
12. You my God ordained spouse, where ever you are, whoever you are, appear and locate me by fire, now, in the name of Jesus.
13. I refuse to settle for less than God's best for me in marriage
14. Every man or woman from any past relationship refusing to let me go and fulfill my God ordained marital destiny, *release me and let me go.* (Say repeatedly the words in italics)
15. Every evil tongue speaking against my God ordained marriage, wither.
16. Let every rebellion flee from my heart in the name of Jesus.
17. Let every rebellion flee from the heart of my God ordained partner.
18. Let the spirit of love, joy, fulfillment, and understanding prevail between me and my partner.
19. This year I shall sing my song, dance my dance, and write my story in the name of Jesus.

20. You powers from the waters attacking my marital destiny, your time is up, receive the hook of the Lord, and die.

21. Marine powers assigned to rewrite my marital destiny, fall down and die.

22. Powers assigned to take my marital life back to square one die, in the name of Jesus.

23. Every barrier separating me from my God ordained partner collapse.

24. Every power, personality, and spirit spoiling my name before my divine partner, be arrested by fire, in the name of Jesus.

25. You, my God ordained marriage, your season has come. Appear by fire. Appear now, in the name of Jesus. (Repeat over and over again "Appear by fire. Appear now.")

CHAPTER 6

TOOLS FOR DOING IT RIGHT

God wants His children to succeed in every area of life including marriage. We can see this from the following scriptures:

"Beloved, I wish above all things that thou mayest prosper and be in health, even as thy soul prospereth." 3 John 1:2.

"For I know the thoughts that I think toward you, saith the Lord, thoughts of peace, and not of evil, to give you an expected end." Jeremiah 29:11.

From these scriptures, we can see that God has great plans for our lives. He wants to give us the more abundant life. **John 10:10a**. The devil on the other hand has terrible plans for our lives including our marriage. His agenda is always to kill, steal, and destroy every good thing that God has for us. **John 10:10b.**

God has made certain tools available to us to enable us to carry out His glorious plans for our lives and to successfully fulfill His destiny for our lives. These tools also help us to overcome the devil and his evil plans for our lives. This chapter will equip us on what these tools are and how to use them effectively to move our marital destiny forward.

The tools are made up the weapons of our warfare. **2 Corinthians 10:4.** They also include our spiritual armor. **Ephesians 6:13-17.** They help us to obtain victory in the warfare surrounding our lives and marriage. The Bible clearly tells us that we are not wrestling against human beings but against wicked spiritual forces that are determined to

57

derail God's plans for our lives and marriage. **Ephesians 6:12.** It teaches us that we can only win this ongoing war by using our spiritual weapons because physical weapons are ineffective against such forces.

"For though we walk in the flesh, we do not war after the flesh: (For the weapons of our warfare are not carnal, but mighty through God to the pulling down of strongholds.)" 2 Corinthians 10:3-4.

In our bid to do it God's way this time, the devil will surely launch an all-out war to stop us as part of this war. Therefore, we should master our weapons and not allow ourselves to be caught unawares by any satanic onslaught. The Bible warns us of this in the verse below:

"Lest Satan should get an advantage of us: for we are not ignorant of his devices." 2 Corinthians 2:11.

These weapons will keep us steps ahead of the devil and his cohorts in our bid to get married God's way and in His time.

Our spiritual armor includes the helmet of salvation; the righteousness of God; the shield of faith; the belt of truth; the shoes of the Gospel of peace; and the sword of the spirit which is the word of God. **Ephesians 6:11-18.** The whole armor is held in place by the master key of prayer. We should ensure that our spiritual armor is on daily to avoid defeat. Also, we should ensure that our armor is intact as any tear or opening constitutes an open door that will allow the enemy to come in and successfully attack us.

Our most indispensable spiritual weapons include the word of God; the name of Jesus; the blood of Jesus; the fire of the Holy Ghost; praise and worship; and the power of the Holy Spirit which is also known as the anointing. We will now briefly discuss these weapons.

1. THE WORD OF GOD (PSALM 1:1-3; JOSHUA 1:8; HEBREW 4:12)

APPROPRIATING THE WORD OF GOD

"For the word of God is quick, and powerful, and sharper than any two edged sword, piercing even to the dividing asunder of soul and spirit, and of the joints and marrow, and is a discerner of the thoughts and intents of the heart." Hebrew 4:12.

The scripture above tells us that God's word is not only living and active but it is also supernatural. There are several promises that the Lord has given to His children in His word. These can be found in both the Logos and the rhema word of God. The Logos is the written word of God as presented in sixty-six chapters of the Bible. The rhema word is the "now" word of God which the Holy Spirit gives to us as needed for any given situation. The Bible clearly tells us that God's word is forever settled in heaven. **Psalm 119:89.** It says also, that once spoken, God's word never returns to Him void but goes forth to accomplish the divine purpose for which it was sent. **Isaiah 55:11.**

We can appropriate the promises of God in His word for our lives as long as we are born again and in good standing with God. They are our inheritance in God through Christ. They equip us and help us to deal with the challenges of life. Therefore, we should learn what is written in the word of God concerning marriage and appropriate them for victory in our marital lives.

"For all the promises of God in him are yea, and in him Amen, unto the glory of God by us." 2 Corinthians 1:20.

We should stand on these promises to actualize the great things that God has for us in marriage. Once God says it in His word, all we have to do is believe it, and that settles it. Praise His name forever! Amen! Amen!! And Amen!!!

CONFESSING THE WORD OF GOD

"Say unto them, As truly as I live, saith the LORD, as ye have spoken in mine ears, so will I do to you:" Numbers 14:28.

"For by thy words thou shalt be justified, and by thy words thou shalt be condemned." Matthew 12:37.

We should confess the word of God over every area of our lives. This is because words are creative and you become what you confess.

God Himself spoke the whole universe into being by the power of the spoken words. **Hebrew 1:3b.** As God's children, we also have this ability because the Bible says that we can decree a thing and it will come to pass. **Job 22:28.** The scripture verse quoted above says that our words carry the power to either justify or condemn us. **Matthew 12:37.** This means that what we confess with our mouths determines what happens in our lives. Therefore, we should form the habit of confessing positive things over our lives and marriage daily. Confession brings possession.

In the same vein, we should flee any form of negative confession because they are deadly. This is because as the scripture verse below tells us, life and death are determined by what we speak into our lives:

"Death and life are in the power of the tongue: and they that love it shall eat the fruit thereof." Proverbs 18:21.

The positive confessions that we make over our lives should come from the word of God, both the logos and the rhema. This is because the Bible says that God so much honors His word that He puts it above His name. **Psalm 138:2.** Whatever God shows you about your marital life, simply believe it, claim it, and confess it often over your life. It is that simple. For example, if God has shown you who your spouse is or given you his or her name, then you should daily confess that he or she is your spouse, even though you have not met her or him yet. There is no need to be timid or shy because all you are doing is cooperating with God by reaffirming what He has told you to actualize your marriage. If God says your husband's name is Jonathan, then everyday your confession should go like this: "Lord, I thank you for my husband Jonathan, I pray that today he will locate me by fire in the name of Jesus." It may sound crazy but it works. When God says it, you should believe it, act on it, and leave the rest to God. God has a history of backing up His word and actually hastening to perform them. **Jeremiah 1:12.**

2. THE NAME OF JESUS

"Wherefore God also hath highly exalted him, and given him a name which is above every name: That at the name of Jesus every knee should bow, of things in heaven, and things in earth, and things under the earth; And that every tongue should confess that Jesus Christ is Lord, to the glory of God the Father." Philippians 2:9-11.

The word of God above tells us that the name of Jesus is higher and greater than every other name. That name "Jesus" is not only higher than principalities, powers, might, dominion, and every other name in this world but also in the world to come. **Ephesians 1:20-23.** Jesus's precious name makes it possible for us to get the God best in every area of our lives including marriage because it carries a supernatural anointing. This anointing breaks the yokes and destroys the strongholds preventing us from getting married. These include the yokes and strongholds of marital failure and satanic delay. Say:

By the anointing in the name of Jesus, I bind and break every evil yoke and stronghold working against my marriage.

The name of Jesus is above every other name including witchcraft, marine powers, occult powers, ancestral powers, familiar spirits, failure, sickness, curses, evil covenants, evil decrees and verdicts, satanic judgments, embargos, rejection, shame, reproach, death, and every other power, spirit, or personality hindering or preventing our marriage. At the mention of the name "Jesus" they have no choice but to bow.

In this name, which is greater than every other name, we are able to speak and to receive greater things into our marital lives. Now let us make the following confessions loud and clear.

1. In the wonderful name of Jesus, I receive a better marriage today.
2. In the awesome name of Jesus, I receive a better spouse today.
3. In the supernatural name of Jesus, I receive better things in my life and marriage today."

3. THE BLOOD OF JESUS (HEBREWS 8:6, REVELATION 12:11)

"But now hath he obtained a more excellent ministry, by how much also he is the mediator of a better covenant, which was established upon better promises." Hebrews 8:6.

Our Lord Jesus through His death on the Cross initiated a better covenant which is sealed with the blood of Jesus. The blood of Jesus serves several purposes in the life of a believer. For one thing, it is the most powerful weapon that we have against the enemy and his evil works. It stops the devil on his track as the scripture below tells us:

"And they overcame him (*the devil*) by the blood of the Lamb, and by the word of their testimony; and they loved not their lives unto the death." Revelation 12:11.

The agenda of the devil is always to kill, steal, and destroy. **John 10:10b.** However, God has given us the all potent weapon of the blood of Jesus to overcome this evil agenda in every area of our lives including marriage. Now repeat after me:

1. Blood of Jesus, work for me in my marital life.
2. Blood of Jesus fight my marital battles for me.
3. I lay my marital life on the platform of the blood of Jesus for deliverance, healing, restoration, and transformation.

The blood of Jesus also speaks:

"And to Jesus the mediator of the new covenant, and to the blood of sprinkling, that speaketh better things than that of Abel." Hebrews 12:24.

This blood speaks better things than the blood of Abel. This means that the blood of Jesus can either speak for us or against us. We can invoke the blood of Jesus against the enemies of our marriage and just like the blood of Abel pursued Cain and became a thorn in his flesh, it will begin to pursue the enemies of our marriage to their destruction.

The blood of Jesus can bulldoze every opposition and obstacle blocking our marriage. Today, it is speaking better things into our lives and marital destiny. It is speaking victory, newness, hope. As a result, we will have better marriages, homes, families, breakthroughs, successes, and glory.

Now, let us invoke the blood of Jesus to speak better things into our marriage by making the following confessions loud and clear.

4. THANKSGIVING, PRAISE, AND WORSHIP

"Enter into his gates with thanksgiving, and into his courts with praise: be thankful unto him, and bless his name." Psalm 100:4.

The verse above makes us to know that thanksgiving, praise, and worship are very important weapons in our battle to get married the God prescribed way. The popular adage says that as our praises go up, God rains down His blessings upon us from heaven. Sometimes praising God is a sacrifice as we may not feel like it. But when you feel like that, then know for sure that it is when you need to praise God the most.

The Bible requires us to give thanks in all things. **Ephesians 5:20.** It also encourages us not to be anxious about anything including marital challenges that we are facing but to tell God about them through our prayers and thanksgiving.

DO IT RIGHT THIS TIME

"Be careful for nothing; but in every thing by prayer and supplication with thanksgiving let your requests be made known unto God." Philippians 4:6.

So as we wait on the Lord for our marriage we should not allow discouragement and frustration to cloud our mind. Instead, we should remember God's faithfulness to us in times past, thank Him for it, and know that in this area of marriage also He will be faithful. With that in mind, even in our midnight hour we should emulate Paul and Silas who in their midnight hour chose to praise God. These servants of God were unjustly locked up in a foreign prison but rather than cave in to discouragement and fear, they praised God. Their praises provoked the earthquake of God's deliverance on their behalf and they received their freedom. **Acts 16:25**. Today, as we too take the time to praise and worship God, He will release His earthquake of deliverance on our behalf. Receive your deliverance in Jesus name. No matter how hard and hopeless our marital situation may appear, aggressive praise and worship will usher God into the situation. It will bring down God's awesome presence and power to bear on our behalf. God will then intervene and shatter all the doors that are closed against marriage, and bring our marriages to pass speedily.

As we bring down God's presence with our thanksgiving, praise, and worship now, I know that our Lord Jesus will touch us and bring about a divine change in our marital situation. Receive your marital restoration. Receive your breakthroughs as you sing in Jesus name.

All I need is a touch from Jesus
All I need is a touch from the Lord
All I need is a touch from Jesus
All I need is a touch from the Lord

That is all I need
All I need is a touch from Jesus
All I need is a touch from the Lord
All I need is a touch from Jesus
All I need is a touch from the Lord

CHAPTER 7

PRAYER AND FASTING

The tool of prayer and fasting is one of the most important tools that we have for resolving the challenges that we face in life. This is particularly so in the area of marriage if we want to do it right this time. It is so important that I have separated it from the other tools of doing it right that were mentioned in the previous chapter.

There is power in prayer and fasting. Prayer is a two way communication between God and man. Without it we cannot know the will of God for us and we will be prone to making errors and mistakes.

Our Lord Jesus Christ taught us that stubborn challenges can only be resolved through targeted fasting and prayers:

"And he (Lord Jesus) said unto them, This kind can come forth by nothing, but by prayer and fasting." Mark 9:29.

The Bible commands us to resist the devil and He will flee from us. **James 4:7.** Prayer and fasting are very effective weapons of doing this. We should therefore regularly engage in prayers and fasting for our God ordained marriage to manifest. We should bombard the enemy with targeted prayers until something happens and he is forced to surrender, release our marriage, and flee.

To achieve marital success, God has to be at the center of it all:

"Except the Lord build the house, they labor in vain that build it: except the Lord keep the city, the watchman waketh but in vain." Psalm 127:1.

Prayer is the most powerful way of getting Him there. We should pray and ask for the help of God in actualizing our marriage so that the labor that we have invested in our marital destiny will not be in vain.

We can also ask our Lord Jesus Christ to intercede for us. He is our faithful and eternal High Priest who continuously intercedes for and ministers to us at the throne of God. **Hebrews 9:11.** Even in this area of marriage He is right ready to intercede for us. All we have to do is ask. This will ensure that none can snatch away the wonderful things that He has for us in marriage.

Decisions about marriage are crucial to our well-being and success in life. So we should invest wisely in fasting and prayers for our marriage, our future home, our husband, and our children.

Prayers for our marriage should be well organized and not just half hazard efforts on our part. Specific times should be set apart each week to fast and pray special targeted prayers for our marriage. We should fast, denying ourselves of food, drink, and even water to give these prayers more wings. Some weekends should be blocked off for this.

You should also keep a prayer journal where you record your prayers and the answers and feedback that you get back from God. Write down your dreams and revelations also. Sometimes in your prayer journal write letters to God concerning your situation, including your concerns, desires, hopes, fears, frustrations, expectations, and other things that you want to share with Him. Empty out your heart in prayer letters to God. Watch out for His answers as prayer is a two way communication.

You should also go through a good deliverance ministration program every quarter until you get married. Thereafter, you can go once or twice a year to maintain your deliverance. **(Please see the appendix section for how to go about deliverance).**

We can see a very good illustration of the power of prayer in getting one's God ordained spouse in the way that Abraham went about selecting a wife for his son, Isaac. It provides a super model for anyone that wants to marry in a godly way. Abraham's servant talking about this said:

"And he said unto me, The LORD, before whom I walk, will send his angel with thee, and prosper thy way; and thou shalt take a wife for my son of my kindred, and of my father's house." Genesis 24:40.

The whole process started with prayers and ended with prayers. Abraham, the man of faith, set the process in motion by declaring boldly and with full confidence, God's ability to secure the correct wife for his son Isaac:

"The LORD God of heaven, which took me from my father's house, and from the land of my kindred, and which spake unto me, and that sware unto me, saying, Unto thy seed will I give this land; he shall send his angel before thee, and thou shalt take a wife unto my son from thence." Genesis 24:7.

Thereafter, the whole process of getting a wife for Isaac was sustained with prayers. **Genesis 24:42-51**.

Abraham could have easily taken a wife for his son from among his Canaanite neighbors. However, he did not do that because he wanted to do it right by getting a wife that was acceptable to God and that would be a blessing to his family. He realized that he needed God's assistance to do this. He also knew that prayer was the best way to get God involved so he made prayer a priority.

He picked a trusted servant that he knew would seek God's help through prayers every step of the way and not just rely on his own human judgment. His trust was not misplaced as we can see from the way that the servant went about picking Rebekah as a wife for Isaac. Everything was done prayerfully. He prayed for God to show him His choice of wife for Isaac and then prayed thanksgiving prayers when God answered his prayers by choosing Rebekah. God was involved also in the negotiation with Rebecca's family for her hand in marriage:

"Behold, Rebekah is before thee, take her, and go, and let her be thy master's son's wife, as the LORD hath spoken." Genesis 24:51.

Neither was He left out in the actual giving of Rebekah by her family to her husband as wife. Her family released her with a prayer of blessing. **Genesis 24:59-61.**

We see therefore that just like the marriage of Rebekah and Isaac, prayer should be made a priority every step of the way in a godly marital relationship. This should start with locating your correct partner; and then courtship; getting married; and finally living together as husband and wife. This is because even after you get married, it will take prayers to sustain the marriage and ensure that marital bliss and harmony continues in the home.

We can see this in the marriage of Isaac and Rebekah. Isaac was meditating on God and His word when Rebekah was brought to him. Soon after, their marriage, like most marriages, hit a major storm. They found out that Rebekah was barren. This particular storm is very vicious and has destroyed many marriages. Let us see how they handled it.

Isaac, a man of prayer, interceded for his wife and God heard and answered his prayer. **Genesis 25:20-22.** In the case of Isaac and Rebekah, whose marriage was built on a Godly foundation, their shame and reproach turned to a double blessing as they gave birth to a set of twin boys, Jacob and Esau.

Even so shall our courtship and marriage be, in Jesus name. They shall be full of mega testimonies in the name of Jesus. For our shame we shall indeed have double. Shame and reproach, shall be far away from us and our homes, in the mighty name of Jesus. Sorrow, tears, and untimely death shall be far from us, in Jesus name. Barrenness shall be far from us in Jesus name. This year, not only will we be blissfully married, but we shall experience the joy of having our babies in Jesus name. Receive your God ordained spouse. Receive your babies in Jesus name.

Let us now compare the God model used to secure a wife for Isaac with the way that Jacob and his brother Esau, the children of Isaac, acquired their wives. We will also compare the way that Isaac and Rebekah handled their marital problems to the way that Jacob and Rachel handled theirs.

Jacob did not follow a godly model in securing a wife unlike the way that Isaac's wife was secured for him. Jacob was captivated by Rachel's outward beauty and did not bother to seek God's will through prayers before marrying her. God on the other hand looks at the heart and not physical appearances when making choices. **1 Samuel 16:17b.** It turned out to be a classic case of unequal yoking as Rachel was an unrepentant idol worshipper who worshipped her father's idols until her death. This was despite her husband's plea not to. **Genesis 31:30-35.**

To make matters even worse, Jacob allowed himself to be lured into polygamy as Laban required him to marry Leah as a condition for being allowed to marry Rachel, his true love. Polygamy, which is the concurrent marriage of a man to multiple wives, is expressly forbidden in the Bible. As mentioned earlier it is not doing it right because it is contrary to God's prescribed marriage of "one man, one wife." **Matthew 19:8.** It is usually a license to marital suicide and trans-generational problems.

A marriage that is not resting on the foundation God's principles will end up with problems and will not get the God desired results of a godly marriage such as unity, peace, joy, and fulfillment.

This was exactly the case with Jacob's marriage and home. There was confusion and problems right from the beginning. These problems eventually led to Rachel's premature death. It also led to her son Joseph, Jacob's favorite child, being sold into slavery in Egypt.

Esau, Jacob's twin brother, married in an even worse way than Jacob. Not only did he not pray before picking his wives, but he married from among the enemies of God and his family. He too was a polygamist. **Genesis 21:9-21.** Close your eyes and pray like this:

1. **I will not marry my enemy in the name of Jesus.**
2. **In this area of marriage, I refuse to be my own problem.**
3. **You my marital destiny refuse to be diverted**
4. **Every power pushing me into the wrong marriage, fail and die.**

These are serious issues that we have discussed above. We should learn from them and seek God in prayer each step of our marital journey until we are successfully married and even beyond. Throughout the process, our watch words and song should be like the songwriter's, "I must tell Jesus." Take everything to God in prayer. We should pray for divine revelation concerning the marriage; pray against satanic delay of our marital breakthrough; pray against the spirit of error and mistake;

69

witchcraft manipulation; ancestral spirit manipulation; and untimely death that can cut short our marital joy or even prevent us from getting married at all.

You should feel free to ask for God's help. **Hebrews 4:16.** He always replies. Never forget He is the Helper of the Helpless, Our Comforter, Our Rescuer, who is ever ready to make a way out of loneliness, shame, reproach, rejection, and other challenges related to our marital lives. Open up to Him. Remember God knows everything so nothing is too shameful or private to discuss with Him. If you cannot speak it out because it is too painful, shameful, or unimaginable, then write it to Him. He can read you know!!!! Even though He knows all things, He would love to hear from you today. Now take this hymn with me. Let it minister to you what a great friend we have in Jesus.

What a Friend we have in Jesus, all our sins and griefs to bear!
What a privilege to carry everything to God in prayer!
O what peace we often forfeit, O what needless pain we bear,
All because we do not carry everything to God in prayer.

Have we trials and temptations? Is there trouble anywhere?
We should never be discouraged; take it to the Lord in prayer.
Can we find a friend so faithful who will all our sorrows share?
Jesus knows our every weakness; take it to the Lord in prayer.

Are we weak and heavy laden, cumbered with a load of care?
Precious Savior, still our refuge, take it to the Lord in prayer.
Do your friends despise, forsake you? Take it to the Lord in prayer!
In His arms He'll take and shield you; you will find a solace there.

Blessed Savior, Thou hast promised Thou wilt all our burdens bear
May we ever, Lord, be bringing all to Thee in earnest prayer.
Soon in glory bright unclouded there will be no need for prayer
Rapture, praise and endless worship will be our sweet portion there.

CHAPTER 8

MARRIAGE AND THE HOLY SPIRIT

Please take this song with me as we invite the Holy Spirit afresh into every area of our lives including marriage:

Spirit of the living God
O fall afresh on me
Spirit of the living God
Fall afresh on me
Mold me, melt me,
Fill me and use me
Spirit of the living God
O fall afresh on me

"But the Comforter (Helper), which is the Holy Ghost, whom the Father will send in my name, he shall teach you all things, and bring all things to your remembrance, whatsoever I have said unto you." John 14:26.

The church of Jesus Christ is currently walking in the dispensation of the Holy Spirit, who is the third person of the God head. He has a huge role to play in our getting married the God ordained way, to the right person, and at the right time. The Holy Spirit He must be involved in every godly marriage. He not only knows our needs but He also knows how to meet these needs. **John 14:26.** He teaches us all things and reveals all things to us, including those things that are yet to happen.

He is the Master Detective who reveals to us the deep secrets that we need to know to move our marital destinies forward. He can take a person with the most messed up marital life, clean it up, and use it to advertise a wonderful marriage for the world to see. The Bible says that the foolishness of God is wiser that the wisest of men. **1 Corinthian 1:25.** It also tells us that God uses the foolish things to confound the wise. **1 Corinthian 1:26-27.** Therefore, the Holy Spirit is able to turn a fool into a wise man in the area of life including marriage.

When the Holy Spirit is invited into a marital relationship, that which should have ended in shame, reproach, disgrace, or disaster, is miraculously turned around and becomes the best marriage. This is similar to what happened at the wedding at Cana, the first wedding that is recorded in the Bible. The celebrants ran out of wine and something had to be done fast to save them from shame and embarrassment. Lord Jesus was invited into the situation at that critical moment. He intervened and turned their mess into a miracle by turning water into wine. **John 2:1-10.** That shall be your portion as the Holy Spirit intervenes on your behalf this season in the name of Jesus.

Scripture says that as many as are led by the Spirit of God, they are the sons of God. **Romans 8:14.** The Holy Spirit not only guides us into the right marriage but He also helps us to sustain it. He never makes mistakes so we can entrust to Him the vehicles of our marital destinies. As God's children, we are His workmanship, so we should allow him to guide us and teach us the way of life. He holds all the information that we need to do it right this time around in the area of marriage:

"But God hath revealed them unto us by his Spirit: for the Spirit searcheth all things, yea, the deep things of God." 1 Corinthians 2:10.

We should not be like Samson who rejected the godly advice of his parents not to be unequally yoked in marriage to unbelievers. He chose his own wayward way instead, moving from one ungodly relationship to another. This eventually led to his glorious destiny being cut short as he died with his enemies after two disastrous marital relationships.

Unlike Samson, who ignored his godly parents, we cannot afford to ignore the all wise voice of the Holy Spirit and His divine counsel for our lives either directly or through God's servants and other authority figures that God has put over us. If we do, the result could be just as catastrophic as Samson's. **Judges 16:1-31.**

The Bible tells us that a person who is often corrected but refuses to take the correction will end up being suddenly destroyed. **Proverbs 29:1.** It also warns us of a way that may seem right to us but that will eventually lead to death and destruction.

"There is a way that seemeth right unto a man, but the end thereof are the ways of death." Proverbs 16:25.

These are strong warnings but they are put there to save us from making a ship wreck of our lives and marital destiny. Today, if you are already on such a road and you have been ignoring the people that God in His mercy has been sending to warn you, you should turn back from such an unprofitable marital relationship. Why have your destiny wasted like Samson's? Let go and God will bring you a better choice: His own choice.

Today, you may be like Samson struggling with a major weakness in your life where the flesh is still reigning. You should not sweep it under the carpet but confront it now. **2 Corinthians 6:2.** The Holy Spirit who is our ever present help in time of trouble is here to help you now. You should confess your weaknesses to God and ask for His grace and mercy. Then ask the Holy Spirit to help you to overcome the weakness. **Romans 5:5.** You should willing to do whatever He asks you to do to fix the problem. **Isaiah 1:18-19.** If you do not, it can mar your marital destiny.

The Holy Spirit is omnipresent so He knows where, how, and when to locate the correct spouse that we need and to bring him or her to us. He is omnipotent so He is able to save, deliver, heal, restore, and transform our lives. He is omniscient so He knows and can reveal to us all the secrets that we need to know to get married and to make a success of it.

He is the power of God that raised Our Lord Jesus from the dead so He is able to bring back to life the good things that have died in our marital lives. **Romans 8:11, Ephesians 1:19-20.**

73

To top all these attributes, the Holy Spirit is very loving and desires the very best for us. He is the greatest Counselor there is. **John 14:26.** We should go directly to Him first and seek His counsel concerning our marital lives before seeking counsel from anyone else. We should not under any circumstances go to quack "prophets" to tell us whom God has ordained for us to marry. We should go directly to God, the source of all revelations and wisdom, for our information:

"The secret things belong unto the LORD our God: but those things which are revealed belong unto us and to our children forever, that we may do all the words of this law." Deuteronomy 29:29.

If we ask God the Father through His Son Jesus, then He will reveal it to us through the Holy Spirit. Our total obedience to the instructions of the Holy Spirit will single us out for marital favor, breakthroughs, excellence, and bliss, in Jesus name. He will not just give us any spouse but an exceptional one that He has custom made for us in Jesus name.

I remember being manipulated into a relationship in Africa some years ago through false prophecies by wolves in sheep clothing within the church. When I sought the Lord's face, He told me that marrying the man would be counterproductive. While still procrastinating, God in His mercy and by His Spirit, intervened by telling a sister in another continent all that He had already told me in Africa. She called me and confirmed all that the Holy Spirit had told me. This enabled me to end the relationship which in turn prevented me from wrecking my life and marital destiny.

Yet several so called "men and women of God" told me that this man was God's ordained choice for me in marriage. This is a great illustration of how dangerous it is to rely on others rather than the Holy Spirit when choosing a spouse. You should go directly to God in prayers yourself. Can you imagine what would have happened if I had not sought God directly for myself and I had believed the lying "prophets"?

These things are serious brethren and should be taken as such. Our very lives and destinies are at stake. We thank God for the Holy Spirit who reveals all things to us. We should listen to Him, take His revelations and counsel to us seriously, and take prompt actions when necessary without procrastinating. We should follow His instructions to the letter, turning neither to the right nor to the left. **Isaiah 30:21.**

Therefore, let us endeavor to listen to the Holy Spirit as we embark on our marital journey. We cannot miss it if we listen to Him and follow His instructions. We must refuse to compromise or yield to pressure from others. I pray that we will not miss it this time around in the mighty name of Jesus. Affliction will not arise a second time in our marital lives in the name of Jesus.

DO IT RIGHT THIS TIME

PRAYERS TO RECEIVE DIVINE WISDOM FOR MARRIAGE

Songs: 1. Breathe on me. 2. Holy Spirit, move me now.
 3. Holy Ghost, connect me to my miracles.

1. Father Lord, forgive me for every sin, disobedience, and rebellion.
2. Holy Spirit, breathe on me.
3. Holy Ghost fire, incubate me and burn away everything that is hindering my marriage.
4. I receive divine wisdom for my marriage.
5. Holy Spirit, restore my spiritual eyes and ears.
6. O Lord, show me beneficial secrets that will move my life forward, in the name of Jesus.
7. Every secret behind my marital problems be revealed unto me.
8. Holy Spirit, give me revelations that will put me at the right place at the right time.
9. Holy Spirit, You are my helper, help me to fulfill my marital destiny.
10. Holy Spirit, please correct me whenever I am about to make a mistake.
11. Holy Spirit, if I have made a mistake, help me to correct it.
12. Holy Spirit, please do not allow me to miss it this time around in the area of marriage.
13. Holy Spirit, by the power by which you raised up Jesus from the dead, raise up every good thing that has died in my marital life.
14. By the power of the Holy Spirit, affliction shall not arise again in my marital life in the name of Jesus.
15. Anointing of the Holy Spirit, fall upon my life and break every yoke preventing my marital life from moving forward.
16. Holy Spirit make my life whole again in the name of Jesus.
17. Holy Spirit glue me together where I am opposed to myself.
18. Holy Spirit, please locate my correct spouse and connect me to him or her.
19. Holy Spirit, move my marital life forward by fire.
20. Holy Spirit, please help me to do it right this time.

CHAPTER 9

MARRIAGE AND YOUR FOUNDATION

Please close your eyes and pray these prayers:

1. I rise above my foundation by the power in the blood of Jesus.
2. Every power carrying evil sacrifice to bury my marital glory and to delay my miracles, be roasted by fire, in the name of Jesus.

Your foundation is your source or your root. It is the pillar on which your life is standing. If it is faulty, every area of your life will be impacted negatively. Therefore, your foundation is a basic fundamental area that you should ensure is properly cleaned up and strengthened if you want to succeed in any area of life especially marriage. In addressing this area which has wasted a lot of destinies and destroyed innumerable marriages and homes, the Bible asks a very troubling question below:

"If the foundation be destroyed what can the righteous do?" Psalm 11:3

Foundational problems are stubborn and difficult to deal with. They can doom a marital relationship from the very beginning if not properly handled. It takes a lot of discipline; prayers; knowledge and application of God's word; commitment; and patience to resolve and overcome them. You should address them before committing to any kind of marital relationship. This is necessary because marriage is a union of two persons so problems brought into the marriage by one partner are shared with the other partner. Marriage in effect magnifies these problems. Besides, any foundational problems that are left unresolved by the couple are eventually transferred to their children.

There are certain symptoms that indicate that there are foundational problems that need to be resolved in a person's life. These include slippery blessings; serious battles at the edge of breakthroughs; failure at the edge of breakthroughs; constant disappointments in marital relationships; satanic delay of blessings; lateness in goodness; acidic poverty; laboring for others to enjoy; diversion of blessings; collective captivity; destiny vandalization; and terrible dream attacks. Another symptom is marital instability.

We will now discuss these foundational problems and how to resolve them.

IDOLATRY (JUDGES 6:25-32)

God hates idol worship with a passion. **Leviticus 26:1; Isaiah 44:6-18**. A past or present background of idolatry brings a family under collective captivity bondage. This opens the door for the devil to come in to kill, steal, and destroy. These doors should be closed with proper repentance, prayers, and deliverance. In addressing the evil idols of our family, we should not be like that brother who said that he gave the idols that he inherited from his father to his uncle to maintain for him while he pursued his job as a "pastor." Instead, we should follow the example of Gideon and deal decisively and courageously with the evil altars of our father's house and the satanic priests that maintain them. **Judges 6:25-32**. These evil priests renew the covenants that keep idol worship in place in our families.

EVIL FAMILY PATTERNS (Colossians 2:14-15)

These are evil trends in a family that keep repeating themselves from one generation to another. They are perpetuated by ancestral and familiar spirits that repeat evil occurrences in a family. An evil pattern could be late or no marriage; divorce; polygamy; adultery; perversion; insanity; cheating; anger; lying; untimely death; or marrying wrong people. For example, in some families everyone marries a witch or wizard.

DO IT RIGHT THIS TIME

In the Bible we see evil patterns in operation in Abraham's family. These included evil pattern of lying and of barrenness. **Genesis 20:2-13; Genesis 26:1-10**. The wives of Abraham, his son Isaac, and his grandson Jacob, were barren. **Genesis 21:1-3; Genesis 25:21.** In David's family, it was sexual looseness. David impregnated Uriah's wife and had him murdered in a bid to cover it up. **2 Samuel 11.** His son Ammon slept with his half-sister Tamar and her brother, Absalom killed him out of revenge. **2 Samuel 13:10-19.** Absalom slept with his father, David's concubines in full view of all Israel. **2 Samuel 16:22.** David's son Solomon, who succeeded him on the throne, set an all-time record by having 700 wives and 300 concubines. **1 Kings 11:1-6.**

From the examples above, we can see that evil patterns if not addressed with the urgency that it requires progressively gets worse. Evil patterns should be bound and broken using the scripture **Colossians 2:14-15**. They should be dis-patterned through aggressive and prolonged prayer bombardment. Once evil patterns are broken, you should then barricade your life and destiny with the blood of Jesus and the fire of the Holy Ghost so that the evil patterns do not creep back in.

PRAYERS TO BREAK EVIL PATTERNS

Song: Blood of Jesus, the blood that conquers satan

1. Cover yourself with the precious blood of Jesus.
2. Confess your sins and those of your ancestors.
3. Apply the blood of Jesus to break all evil covenants and curses keeping evil patterns in place in your life.
4.   (a) Let the fire of God go deep into my foundation and purge everything that is feeding evil patterns in my life and marital destiny.
**   (b) Blood of Jesus flush them out. Take time to pray this very well.**
5. Every strongman enforcing evil patterns in my life, fall down and die.

6. Every evil door and gate permitting evil patterns to operate in my life, be closed by the blood of Jesus.

7. Use the under listed (a-o) to fill in the blank space below:
Every evil family pattern of ....be dis-patterned by the blood of Jesus.

a. Premature death	b. Divorce	c. Mental disease	d. Hatred
e. Disappointment	f. Rejection	g. Reproach	h. Bareness
i. Confusion	j. Sickness	k. Oppression	l. Poverty
m. Looseness with opposite sex		n. Perversion	o. Abortion

8. Where is the Lord God of Elijah? Arise and let my matrimonial story change, in the name of Jesus.

9. Every voice of the stranger speaking against my marital life and destiny, shut up, in the name of Jesus.

10. Every power, spirit, and personality, in my foundation that is working against my marital breakthrough, be uprooted and die.

11. Lay your right hand on your head and repeat 21 times, "I say no, no, no to every pattern of inherited marital failure."

12. Every evil river flowing into my life from my foundation, dry up.

14. Every evil ladder keeping evil patterns in place in my life, catch fire and burn to ashes, in the name of Jesus.

13. Every evil river in my place of birth or origin troubling my marital destiny, I pollute you with the blood of Jesus.

14. Pick from the under listed (a-s) and say,
"You evil pattern of ......, you are not my portion, break and die, in the name of Jesus." (Repeat this three hot times)

a. Lateness in marriage	b. Failure at the edge of breakthroughs	
c. Marital failure	d. Wrong partner	e. Confusion
f. Marital disappointment	g. No marriage	h. use and dump
i. Untimely death	j. Evil spiritual marriage	
k. Insanity	l. Evil dreams	m. Frustration
n. Marital rejection	o. Fornication	p. Adultery
q. Marital distress	r. Rising and falling	s. Divorce

HOUSEHOLD WICKEDNESS POWERS

"And a man's foes shall be they of his own household." Matthew 10:36.

The preceding scripture, teaches us that a man's worse enemies are the members of his own household. There are several examples of this in the Bible. Proverbial examples are Joseph's wicked brothers who sold him into slavery in Egypt out of envy. Their goal was to terminate his colorful destiny but God had different plans. **Genesis 37:12-36; Genesis 50:20.** Joseph running his mouth had shared with them the glorious dreams that he had about his future. Who are you sharing your dreams with? Beware! There are vision killers around and most of them are in your own family.

Another example is Abraham who made no significant progress in life until he totally obeyed God and separated himself completely from his father's house. This included separation from his nephew Lot, who had become a burden, weighing down his progress. **Genesis 13:6-18.**

To make marital progress we have to like Abraham sever all spiritual linkage to the evil powers of our father's house and our mother's house. This is even more urgent if you constantly have dreams of being back in your father's house or in the house where you grew up.

In the physical as well, you have to be very careful in your dealings with your family members, particularly if they are not born again. This is because the devil can easily use them as weapons to truncate your life and marital destiny. **Matthew 10:36.**

PRAYERS TO OVERCOME HOUSEHOLD
WICKEDNESS POWERS

1. Bring quality repentance before God for yourself and your ancestors.
2. Blood of Jesus separate me from the sins of my ancestors.
3. Every evil power pursuing me from my father's house, die.
4. Every evil power pursuing me from my mother's house, die.
5. Every power making me not to be what God says that I am, die.
6. Every power making me to be what God says that I am not, die.

7. Every evil power of my father's house saying no to God's yes for my life and marriage, die.

8. Every evil tree housing my marital goodness, release it, dry up and die, in the name of Jesus.

9. Household witchcraft powers hear the word of the Lord, remove your dirty hand from the affairs of my life and marriage.

10. Household wickedness powers assigned to manipulate me into a wrong marriage, you are liars, therefore release me and die.

11. Household wickedness powers assigned to uproot me from the company of the married you have a failed, release me and let me go.

12. Every fetish power working against my marital destiny, die.

13. Where is the Lord God of Elijah? Arise and fight for me.

14. Every effect of any evil transmission into my life through strange touches, hugs, or kisses, both in the dream and in the physical, be removed by the blood of Jesus.

15. All unprofitable broadcasters of my marital goodness, be silenced by the blood of Jesus.

16. Thunder of God, destroy the power operating any spiritual vehicle working against my life and marriage.

17. I destroy every evil peace, evil agreement, evil unity, evil love, evil happiness, evil understanding, evil communication, evil reconciliation, and evil gathering fashioned against my marriage.

18. Every evil car and driver reversing my marital destiny backwards, catch fire and be roasted to ashes.

19. Thou power of polygamous witchcraft working against my life and marriage, die.

20. Evil hands and legs militating against my marriage, I cut you off now. (Demonstrate this using the sword of God to cut them off.)

21. Parental curses working against my life and marriage, break.

22. Blood of Jesus, reverse the effect of every evil manipulation of my hair, clothing, menstrual pad, under wears, and other personal effects, upon my life and marriage.

23. I turn back from every evil marital journey that household wickedness powers have ordained for me in the name of Jesus.

24. I recover back everything that household wicked powers have stolen from me by the power in the blood of Jesus.

ANCESTRAL POWERS (EXODUS 20:3-4; JOSHUA 24:14-15)

Ancestral powers are the evil powers that carry over family problems from one generation to another. They transmit evil bondages through the bloodline. There are negative covenants that keep these powers and the problems associated with them in place. When these covenants are broken, curses kick in. There are also ancestral strongmen that supervise these problems in the lives of family members from one generation to another.

Ancestral powers marry off family members to the particular deity that a family worships in the spirit realm. Such idols include serpents, water, and other elements. As long as these spiritual marriages are in place they will hinder family members from getting married in the physical realm. Ancestral spirits also seek to confuse and divert people by pushing them into marriages with wrong partners that God has not ordained for them. We should resist and refuse every attempt by these powers to divert our marital destiny.

Ancestral powers monitor the lives of their victims using evil devices such as evil marks, plantations, deposits, tattoos, and incisions. This enables them to know when good things are coming to their victims and they promptly swing into action to abort or divert them before they manifest.

They launch attacks against their victims from evil ancestral altars which are maintained by designated satanic priests in the family. These altars remain actively indefinitely until they are killed through deliverance. Even when the priest maintaining the altar dies and the altar is physically pulled down, the altar remains active spiritually and continues to demand for worship and manipulate the lives of family members. Altars can only be destroyed using spiritual means. **2 Corinthians 10:4**. Pray the following prayers like a mad prophet.

1. Every altar fighting against my marital breakthroughs, scatter unto desolation, in Jesus name.

2. Every evil priest ministering at such altars, fall down and die.

Some years back I met a young man, who was a very talented praise and worship leader. His father pastored a big church in town. He told me that he wanted to marry me. He sang well and appeared very devoted to me. I started having dreams about a man that was trying to rape me. I took his name and the situation to my pastor, who gave me prayers to pray. As I prayed them, the Lord opened my eyes to see what was really going on.

In the revelation, I saw myself in the compound where I grew up. There, I saw my grandmother who died fifteen years earlier but was alive in this dream. She arrived in a car and said that my parents had instructed her to bring me to a man for marriage. I knew right away that I must not go with her. I took off running and she pursued me. As I ran, I kept shouting "You cannot force me to marry a man that God has not ordained for me to marry." I tried to escape through one gate but she closed it before I could. Then I ran to the second gate which was manned by two of my friends who tried to help her catch me. I dashed past them and escaped before any of them could catch me. I woke up still shouting: "You cannot force me to marry whom God has not ordained for me to marry." Close your eyes and pray this prayer for yourself:

1. I will not marry anyone that God has not ordained for me to marry.
2. Every power assigned to make me do so, fall down and die now.

My grandmother in the dream represented ancestral powers while my parents represented household wickedness powers. The friends were unfriendly friends. All three groups mentioned above are close enemies.

Within two weeks that whole relationship ended abruptly. That was how I escaped a bad marriage that ancestral powers had arranged for me. Thank God for the sweet escape that the Holy Ghost orchestrated for me that day. So shall you escape every trap and snare set for you in the area of marriage, in the name of Jesus. You shall not marry your enemy in the name of Jesus.

Ancestral powers are also adept at manipulating people's dreams and visions. They use them to manipulate such people into wrong

84

relationships by presenting their friends as their enemies and their enemies as their friends. They make bad relationships appear good. This is particularly true for those that have never gone for deliverance or whose deliverance is not complete. They are agents of destiny diversion and destruction. God will indeed deliver us from their hands in the mighty name of Jesus. Make the following declaration loud and clear:

My dreams and imagination will not be used against me in the name of Jesus.

We will now look at various ways that ancestral powers can hinder a person's marital destiny.

EVIL DEDICATION

People, places, houses, ministries, businesses, careers and even marriages, can be dedicated to God. On the other hand, they can be dedicated to satan and his evil powers. **Numbers 6:27, 1 Samuel 1:20-28.** An evil dedication is to consecrate or devote a person, a thing, or a place to the worship of any deity or power other than Jehovah God. It is to be set apart for any other spiritual purpose apart from Jehovah's. It could be dedication to an idol, a shrine, or an evil spirit.

Evil dedication is a major tool used by ancestral powers and household wickedness powers to lay claims on and manipulate people's lives. Idol worshipper's dedicate their lives and possessions including their children, even those yet unborn, to the idols that they serve. These idols could be animals such as crocodile, cows, and snakes; water spirits; trees; forest demons; or witchcraft powers.

The spiritual implication of this is that you are sold off to any power to which you are dedicated. This in effect makes you their property and their slave. Also, you are married to any power that you are dedicated to. This is similar to Christians who are dedicated to Jesus Christ and married to Him. **Ephesians 5:31-32. Numbers 25:3-5.** Your ancestors are deemed to have received a dowry on your head from all the benefits that they received from these idols. Your life was indeed used as collateral or a down payment, for receiving those benefits which include wealth, protection, children, bountiful harvest, good health, and victory over their enemies.

These evil transactions give these evil powers unlimited access to a person's life and destiny. You remain their slave until you nullify the evil marriage and sale by using the blood of Jesus to buy your life back and to break the evil covenants keeping the dedication in place.

Evil covenants with ancestral powers are reinforced in various ways. These include eating food offered to them; attending ceremonies and festivals organized to honor them; and through demonic sacrifices offered to them. They are also reinforced through evil touches, hugs, kisses, sex, swimming, and eating in the dream or in the physical.

Ancestral powers are very possessive and jealous and want you to remain married to them so they seriously oppose your marry anyone else in the physical.

There are ancestral strongmen that enforce these evil covenants. It takes the blood of Jesus to break the evil covenants binding you to them. Today you should break all such covenants. **Colossians 2:14-15.** You also have to break all the covenanted curses that come with the evil dedication. **Galatians 3: 13-14.** Lastly, you should pray for God to restore all that you have lost as a result of the evil dedication. **Joel 2:25.** Please prayer the following prayers with boiling anger in your spirit:

1. **I refuse to pay for what I did not buy, in the name of Jesus.**
2. **Every ancestral debt collector forcing me to pay for what I did not buy, you are a liar, die, now.**
3. **Blood of Jesus, buy me back from every power to which I have been sold, in the name of Jesus.**
4. **Blood of Jesus nullify every marriage between me and any idol, in the name of Jesus.**

The sad thing is that most people are not even aware that they have been covenanted to these wicked powers by their ancestors. Neither are they aware that their lives are being manipulated and controlled by them.

A woman attended deliverance in one of our churches. During the deliverance, there was a prophetic word about a sister that was married to a serpent. She never suspected that her inability to get married in the physical was because she was married to the family idol, a serpent. However, on getting home a huge snake lay dead on her bed. The snake had been sleeping with her on her bed every night in the spirit but she never knew until her eyes were opened. Soon after that she got married. Praise the Lord. God is good.

Today, if you are under this kind of bondage, the Lord will do the same for you. He will open your eyes to see your true position and set you free, in Jesus name. Your own case will not be different. Receive your deliverance in the name of Jesus.

EVIL NAMES

Names are very important to God. They are so important that He changed the names of several people in the Bible to enable them fulfill their divine destiny. A good example is Jacob. His name meant trickster and it caused him a lot of trouble. These problems continued until God changed it to "Israel" which means "One that prevails with God and man." **Genesis 32:28.**

An evil name is any name that does glorifies the devil rather than God. It is any name that subtracts from a person's destiny rather than adding value to it. An evil name defiles a person's destiny. Some names are given under the influence of ancestral spirits and in honor of ancestral powers. Such names magnetize troubles to their bearers in all areas of life including marriage. For example, bearing a name that means "I belong to the water idol," will constitute an evil load and weigh down your destiny and marital progress. When you belong to an idol, you are set aside for the idol's use. You are dedicated to the idol and in effect married to it. Until this evil marriage is properly renounced, revoked, and broken spiritually, it will be impossible to get married successfully in the physical. You need to take the initiative or God will allow the evil name to continue weighing down your life and marriage, until you get wise and get rid of it.

Even more importantly, until you change that evil name that you are carrying around, you cannot profit in your trading with God in any area of life including marriage. This is because God is a jealous God and is not willing to share His glory with any power including family idols. **Exodus 20:5-7**.

This is a very serious matter. You truly have to choose this day who you will serve. Are you going to serve the living God or are you going to serve idols? **Joshua 24:15.** The name that you are carrying around tells the true story. How can you say that you belong to Jesus when your name tells the whole world that you belong to the devil and his agents? How can you fear your family or an idol more than you fear God? Like Apostle Paul said, "How can you drink from the cup of devils and also drink from the cup of our Lord Jesus?" **1 Corinthians 10:21.**

If your name is polluted or glorifies the devil you should prayerfully change it. Until you do that, your whole life including marriage, cannot move forward. God cannot pour His Spirit, power, glory, and favor into such a life when the person is dishonoring God by being too weak, fearful, undiscerning, and spiritually immature to drop an evil name in order to align his life to God's purpose and destiny for his life.

This issue goes back to the maturity and readiness for marriage that we talked about earlier in the book. If you cannot get your own life in order then how do you want to get married to someone else and succeed at it?

PRAYERS AGAINST EVIL DEDICATION

1. Bring quality repentance before the Lord for your sins and those of your ancestors.
2. Let the power in the blood of Jesus separate me from the sins of my ancestors.
3. Every evil dedication over my life, break and die in the name of Jesus.
4. Every power saying no to God's yes for me in marriage die.
5. All ancestral debt collectors forcing me to pay for what I did not buy, die now.
6. Every ancestral strongman enforcing evil dedication in my life, fall down and die.
7. I break and loose myself from every inherited evil covenant and curse, in Jesus' name.

8. Every evil dedication, lose your hold over my life and be purged out of my foundation, in the name of Jesus.

9. I renounce and loose myself from any evil dedication placed upon my life, in Jesus' name.

10. I command all demons associated with any broken evil parental vow and dedication to depart from me now, in the name of Jesus.

11. Let the evil consequences of any broken demonic promise or dedication upon my life, be cancelled by the power in the blood of Jesus.

12. Thou power of spiritual dowry I bind you, break and release me by fire.

13. I take authority over all the curses emanating from any broken dedication over my life, in Jesus' name.

14. Every evil yoke with ancestral powers, break and release me now.

15. Every power troubling my marital life, die in the name of Jesus.

16. Blood of Jesus redeem my life from every power to which I have been sold.

17. Every evil family history that wants to repeat itself in my life and marriage, die now, in the name of Jesus.

18. Any power in my foundation assigned to make my marriage fail, fall down and die now.

19. I rededicate myself to God, in the name of God the Father, and of the Son, and of the Holy Spirit.

20. Thank you Lord for answering my prayers.

EVIL ANCESTRAL PLANTATION (See a more detailed discussion in the section on witchcraft)

"As soon as they hear of me, they shall obey me: the strangers shall submit themselves unto me. The strangers shall fade away, and be afraid out of their close places." Psalm 18:44-45.

Evil plantations are evil products planted in a person's body and spirit by the enemy. Evil ancestral plantations are evil ancestral deposits that flow down through the blood line. They are evil strangers that must be chased out of their hiding places by the fire of God and flushed out by the blood of Jesus. **Psalm 18:44-45.** Some are planted right from a person is in his or her mother's womb. They act as evil monitors that trigger problems every time a good thing, including marriage, is coming a person's way. For example, they can make a person run mad when it is time to get married, during the wedding ceremony, or after child birth.

Some entry points of evil ancestral plantations are incisions, tattoos, and marks. Another is evil food eaten from wrong people and in the wrong places such as partaking of polluted food in parties or in ancestral festivals dedicated to idols. Ancestral powers also reinforce evil ancestral plantations and deposits through dreams. One way is through sex with ancestral spirit spouses in the dream. Another is through eating, kissing, and hugging in the dream. They also come in through cuts, scratches, and bites the dreams. These include human, dog, serpent, and scorpion bites.

You should get rid of evil ancestral plantations through deliverance. Only the fire of God and the blood of Jesus can purge away and flush out evil plantations and deposits.

PRAYERS TO UPROOT ANCESTRAL PLANTATION
1. Every evil product in my body I challenge you with the fire of God, be flushed out by the blood of Jesus.
2. Every plantation of defilement in my body, come out.
3. Every evil thing working against my marriage, be uprooted and return back to sender.

90

COLLECTIVE CAPTIVITY (Galatians 3:13-14; Colossians 1:13; Colossians 2:15; 2 Timothy 4:18).

"Wherefore he saith, When he ascended up on high, he led captivity captive, and gave gifts unto men." Ephesians 4:8.

Collective captivity is when the members of a group of people such as a family, a city, or a tribe are under the same bondages. Covenants and curse keep these in place. They could all be operating under a common curse, spell, bewitchment, or sickness. They all face similar problems and challenges in life. For example all the men from a particular family or town may have low sperm count, which renders them impotent and infertile. The women may be beautiful and prosperous yet no man wants to marry them. It could be that most people from a particular city are sexually loose or are drunkards.

A biblical example is the collective perversion that obtained in Sodom and Gomorrah. It eventually brought down God's judgment which led the city and its inhabitants being destroyed. **Genesis 19**.

From the discussion above we see that the consequences of collective captivity can be devastating. Therefore, you should prayerfully find out the source of the problem that is plaguing your family; confess your sins and those of your ancestors; and pray targeted prayers to separate yourself from the evil family umbrella and set yourself free. You should also use the blood of Jesus to separate yourself from every collective captivity vehicle of your father's house that is carrying you where God has not ordained for you to go and set it on fire.

You can also go for deliverance ministration. Always remember that even the captive of the mighty and the terrible can be delivered.

"Shall the prey be taken from the mighty, or the lawful captive delivered? But thus saith the Lord, Even the captives of the mighty shall be taken away, and the prey of the terrible shall be delivered." Isaiah 49:24-25.

No case is too hard for God. **Jeremiah 32:17.** God who is mighty to save and mighty to deliver shall surely deliver you from every bondage, in the mighty name of Jesus.

PRAYERS TO DESTROY COLLECTIVE CAPTIVITY

1. Every evil umbrella preventing my rain of marital joy and fulfillment from falling on me, catch fire in the name of Jesus.
2. Every strongman blocking the sunlight of my marital glory, die.
3. Blood of Jesus, repair and seal up every licking roof over my head.
4. Every door opened by ancestral powers through which the enemy is attacking me, be closed by the blood of Jesus.
5. Press you right index finger on your navel and pray: Every evil spiritual naval gate, through which poison is flowing into my marital destiny, be cut off by the power in the blood of Jesus.
6. By the power of the Holy Ghost, I jump out of every evil collective vehicle of my father's house/mother's house. I command the vehicle and the driver to catch fire and be roasted to ashes.
7. I break every evil edict and ordination over my life and marriage.
8. Every ancestral serpent troubling my destiny stretch and die now.
9. You the belly of the ancestral serpent burst open and vomit every good thing that you have stolen from me, in the name of Jesus.
10. Covenants and curses fueling evil collective captivity in my life and family, break by the blood of Jesus.
11. Blood of Jesus, silence the evil cry of my family idols troubling my marital destiny, in Jesus name.
12. I set ablaze every ancestral altar and priest working against my life and marriage. Burn to ashes, in the name of Jesus.
13. I separate my life and marriage from every evil tree harboring my goodness, and I uproot it and set it on fire, in the name of Jesus.
14. Every ancestral vulture that has swallowed up my life and marriage, vomit me now, in the name of Jesus.
15. Every ancestral curse controlling my life, break and release me by fire.

PRAYERS TO KILL ANCESTRAL DESTROYERS

1. By the power in the blood of Jesus, I break every evil ancestral hold over my marital destiny.

2. Every evil family river flowing into my life, I cut you off, dry up from your source.

3. Thunder of God, locate and destroy every family serpent and idol troubling my life and marriage.

4. Ancestral powers forcing me to marry whom God has not ordained for me to marry, you have failed, die, in the name of Jesus.

5. I escape out of every ancestral cage and trap fashioned against my marriage.

6. Evil ancestral marital patterns in my family, my life is not your candidate, therefore break and die.

7. I break the head of every serpent troubling my life and marriage.

8. Every dark serpent troubling my life and marriage, die now.

9. Every power claiming ownership of my life and claiming to be my spouse, be roasted now, in the name of Jesus.

10. I fire back every arrow fired into my life by my family idols.

11. Every cycle and every pattern of hardship in my family line, break and release me now, in the name of Jesus.

12. Power of God, uproot wicked plantations from my life.

13. Holy Ghost fire, purge my blood of satanic injections and deposits.

14. Every power, personality, and spirit assigned to spoil me for my spouse, fall down and die.

15. Every curse operating in my family line, break by fire.

16. Any voice from the pit of hell contending against my marriage, be silenced by the blood of Jesus.

17. Every venomous poison in my head be purged by fire and flushed out by the blood of Jesus.

18. Every venomous poison in my body, come out now.

19. Every serpent that has swallowed my marital goodness, burst open, vomit it and die, in the name of Jesus.

20. Every damage done to my life and marriage by ancestral powers receive divine solution.

FOUNDATIONAL STRONGMEN
(1 SAMUEL 17, LUKE 11:21-22)

"When a strongman, armed keepeth his palace, his goods are in peace. But when a stronger that he shall come upon him, and overcome him, he taketh from him all his armor in which he trusted, and divideth his spoils." (Luke 11:21-22)

A major force from your foundation to reckon with in the battle against your marriage is the issue of foundational strongmen. These powers dominate and control families. There are both spiritual and physical strongmen in families that can prevent people from getting married. They also push people into wrong marriages, thereby diverting such destinies. Some of these strongmen operate across generations and are known as generational strongmen.

In the spirit, a strongman is the principal demon in charge of a group of demons assigned by the devil to kill, steal, and destroy. It is the huge serpent or millipede that escapes in your dream after you have killed all the others. He is that larger than life person that confronts, opposes, blocks, and oppresses you in your dreams.

The strongman has a warehouse where he locks up the things that he has stolen from people including marriages, wedding garments, husbands, children, body parts, wealth, money, glory, virtues, potentials, and various documents of advancement. **Luke 11:21.** Such documents include marriage certificates, diplomas, contracts, and citizenship papers.

In the physical, a strongman is that wicked parent, step parent, sibling, boss, pastor, uncle, or aunty circulating your name around for evil. They are those evil legs working about for your sake. They are the evil hands planting evil seeds and trees into your life. They are the evil eyes monitoring your life for affliction. They supervise affliction in a person's life. They are those that have sworn that over their dead bodies will you ever get married. Today just as they have spoken so it shall be unto them because it is now time for you to marry in Jesus name. Close your eyes and pray like this:

94

1. Every man or woman (mention their names if you know who they are) saying that over his or her body will I marry, so be it, it is now time for me to marry, therefore, die by thunder.
2. Evil legs and evil hands militating against my marriage, I cut you off with the sword of God. (Imagine you are holding a machete and demonstrate this.)
3. Every satanic surveillance over my life and destiny, be dismantled by the power of God.
4. Every strongman supervising affliction in my life, die.

These strongmen are powerful but Jesus is more powerful. They are strong but Our Lord Jesus is the "Stronger One." **Luke 11:21-22.** He lives in us and makes us strong enough to take on these wicked powers hence the Bible says:

"Greater is he that is in you than he that is in the world." 1 John 4:4.

You should not be afraid of them because Lord Jesus, the Greater One and the Stronger One, lives in you.

To be able to release and take back the things that belong to you from the strongman, you have to first overcome the strongman by binding him in the name of Jesus. **Mark 3:27.** Then you can go in and collect your marital goodness and possession that are in his custody. Let us take this warfare song:

So I go to the enemy's camp
And I take back what he stole from me
I take back what he stole from me
He's under my feet
He's under my feet
Satan is under my feet

Just like the song says, now declare with faith:

I go to the enemy's camp and I snatch back everything that he has stolen from me.

Some of these strongmen manifest as spirit husbands and wives. Sometimes there are generational ancestral or inherited spirit husbands, who are married to all the women in a particular family line. Similarly there are inherited spirit wives who are married to all the men in a family.

If you have dreams of sharing the same man with your children then there is an ancestral spirit husband on the prowl. Your ancestors have married all the women in your family line to him. You have to castrate him and kill him with the Holy Ghost vomited hot prayers at the end of this section.

All the men in a family can also be married off to an ancestral spirit wife that molests them sexually. This could manifest in the physical as impotency and low sperm count making it impossible for them to have children in the physical.

Only our Lord Jesus is able to set you and your possessions free from the clutches of wicked spiritual and physical strongmen, even if you are their lawful captive. **Isaiah 49:24-26.** Just like stubborn Goliath and Pharaoh in the Bible, these strongmen need to die so that your marriage can be released and you can get married and find fulfillment in it. You can kill them with the Holy Ghost vomited prayers in the next section.

DO IT RIGHT THIS TIME

PRAYERS TO OVERCOME AND SPOIL THE STRONGMAN

Song: 1. Strongman, submit your power. 2. So I go to the enemy's camp and I take back what he stole from me.

1. You ancestral strongman, standing at the gate of my marriage to hinder me, fall down and die, in the name of Jesus.
2. Household strongman, assigned against my marital joy, die.
3. Hammer of God, break open every door closed by any strongman to prevent me from entering my land of marital victory and fulfillment.
4. Every generational strongman assigned against my marriage, die now.
5. I take authority over and bind the strongman holding on to my marital blessings.
6. Dynamite power of God break open every strong room and storehouse where the strongman is keeping my marital possessions and release them.
7. I go in and I take possession of all my possessions locked up in the strongman's storehouse, in the name of Jesus.
8. I escape from the cage of the strongman with all my possession, *I escape now.* (Demonstrate this by running out).
9. Every Goliath boasting against my marital life, receive the stones of fire, and die, in the name of Jesus.
10. Every stubborn and unrepentant Pharaoh, pursing my marital destiny for destruction, perish in the Red Sea of your own making.
11. Every man or woman seating on my marital blessings, I strip you of your power, be unseated by fire.
12. I receive power to pursue, overtake, and recover all that the strongman has stolen from my life and marriage.
13. I pursue, I overtake, and I recover all my marital possessions from the hands of every strongman.
14. Evil hands and feet walking about for my sake, be paralyzed.

END OF CHAPTER PRAYERS

1. O God, arise and let all the enemies of my marriage scatter.

2. Holy Ghost fire, blood of Jesus, travel deep into the root of my life and work a deep deliverance in my life and marriage, in the name of Jesus.

3. Evil spirits hiding in my foundation come out now. You ……… (Pick from the under listed) come out and die now in Jesus name.

a. Spirit of rejection	b. Spirit of shame	c. Spirit of poverty
d. Failure	e. Reproach	f. Sickness and disease
g. Nakedness	h. Sorrow and tears	i. Evil marks
j. Ancestral loneliness	k. Evil smell	l. Flies and Beelzebub
m. Evil handwriting	n. Evil labels	o. Insanity

4. Light of God, dispel every darkness in my foundation.

5. Evil plantations from my foundation come out with all your roots and die.

6. Every poison of darkness in my foundation, come out and depart from me.

7. Foundational powers behind my marital problems, I bury you alive.

8. Blood of Jesus separate from me every Lot that is attached to my marital destiny.

9. Every problem programmed to manifest in my marriage in the future, you shall not see the light of day, be aborted now.

10. Every agenda of the wicked to naked my life in the area of marriage, fail and die by fire, die now.

11. Every power mocking God in my marital life, die by fire.

12. Every evil seed and root in my foundation working against my marital fulfillment, be uprooted by fire.

13. Every ancient strongwoman assigned to truncate my marital destiny; your time is up, somersault and die in the name of Jesus.

14. Every strongman in charge of my case, fall down and die.

15. Every ancestral rat assigned against my marriage, die by fire.

CHAPTER 10

MARRIAGE AND WITCHCRAFT

"There shall not be found among you any one that maketh his son or his daughter to pass through the fire, or that use divination, or an observer of times, or an enchanter, or a witch." Deuteronomy 18:10.

Let us take these prayer points:

1. Every witch that comes before me, I bury you now, in the name of Jesus.
2. Every power that is monitoring my marital life for evil and bewitchment, be chained permanently to the bottomless pit, in the name of Jesus.

Witchcraft is a sin which is expressly forbidden by God. **1 Samuel 15:23; Deuteronomy 18:10.** Witchcraft powers seek to manipulate a person to do their will and to follow their satanic agenda as opposed to doing God's will and following His agenda. They directly oppose and attack God's plans, purpose, and timing for a person's life. God hates them with perpetual hatred and has issued a judgment of death on them saying:

"Suffer not a witch to live." Exodus 22:18.

You should not tolerate their activities in any area of your life. You should not waste your time trying to pacify witches but rather return fire for fire and force them to bow. Witchcraft is a craft and witches continuously practice witchcraft to manipulate lives. To counteract this, you should do spiritual warfare against them daily.

There are different types of witchcraft. These include household, environmental, envious, anti-promotion, and marine witchcraft. These powers employ many weapons to fight a person's marital destiny. Their goal is to delay and prevent a person from getting married. These weapons are also used to manipulate a person into marrying the wrong partner or from marrying in the way that God has set forth in His word. These witchcraft weapons will be discussed in the next section. First let us pray the following prayers.

PRAYERS TO KILL THE WITCHCRAFT IN YOUR MARITAL DESTINY

1. Every agenda of household witchcraft for my marriage scatter unto desolation.
2. Wicked birds flying against my marital destiny, fall down, die, and be roasted to ashes, in Jesus' name.
3. Every witchcraft verdict, decision, decree or, vow militating against my getting married, be reversed and nullified by the blood of Jesus.
4. Every witchcraft cage that is caging me or my God ordained partner, break and release us by fire.
5. Every witchcraft power summoning my spirit to any witchcraft coven, perish by fire, in the name of Jesus.
6. Anything representing me and my marriage in any coven, I withdraw your representation and I command you to burn to ashes.
7. Every witchcraft weapon being used against my marriage catch fired and roast to ashes.
8. I reject every witchcraft seat prepared for me to seat on and I set it on fire.
9. I command my enemies to seat on the evil seat that they have prepared for me.
10. I withdraw any mandate given to any witch to afflict me in the name of Jesus.

11. Every witchcraft tongue speaking against my marriage, wither and be cut off by fire.

12. Every power calling my name before evil mirrors, die with your mirror.

13. I pursue, I overtake, and I recover all my possessions in witchcraft covens.

14. You witchcraft powers assigned against my life and marriage I command you to take my place and seat on the seat that you have prepared for me.

WITCHCRAFT SALE OF MARRIAGE

"Woe to the bloody city! It is all full of lies and robbery; the prey departeth not;........the horseman lifted up both the bright sword and the glittering spear: and there is a multitude of slain, and a great number of carcases; and there is none end of their corpses; they stumble upon their corpses: because of the multitude of the whoredoms of the well favored harlot, the mistress of witchcrafts, that selleth nations through her whoredom, and families through her witchcrafts." Nahum 3:1.

Please pray these prayers violently:

1. My marriage is not for sale, in the mighty name of Jesus.

2. My life is not for sale, in the name of Jesus.

3. My family is not for sale, in the name of Jesus.

4. Blood of Jesus, buy me back from every power to which I have been sold.

5. Blood of Jesus, buy my marriage back from every power to which it has been sold.

6. Every witchcraft basket assigned to sell off my marital virtues, catch fire.

7. I set every witchcraft market working against my life and marriage on fire.

A witchcraft sale is a satanic exchange or transfer of virtues from one person to another to prevent such a person from fulfilling his or her God ordained destiny. The God ordained marriage can be sold off and once this happens, a once thriving God ordained relationship is emptied out and if nothing is done about it, it just dies. This is because what should keep the couple attracted to each other; help them to realize God's potential for them as a couple; and help the relationship to thrive has been sold off. This is tantamount to destiny diversion. I pray that the Lord will deliver us from witchcraft traders.

Witchcraft powers can sell the souls, destiny, and virtues of the prospective couple. **Revelation 18:13.** They can sell off the marital victory, fulfillment, and children that God has ordained for the marriage. They can steal a couple's marriage by manipulating one or both of them to marry the wrong person. They can render a couple barren or exchange the good and healthy children that God has ordained for them for bad and sick children. They can steal and sell the things that God ordained to make a marriage blossom, shine, and stand out. We have to watch and pray fervent prayers because the devil never relents. He fights to the end.

PRAYER TO DELIVER YOUR MARRIAGE FROM WITCHCRAFT SALE

1. By the power in the blood of Jesus, I declare that my life is not for sale.
2. By the power in the blood of Jesus, I declare that the life of my God ordained partner is not for sale.
3. By the power of the Holy Ghost, I declare that my marital fulfillment and joy are not for sale.
4. Blood of Jesus buy back my marital virtues, potentials, deposits and marriage from any power to which they have been sold. (Then repeat over and over, "Blood of Jesus buy them back.")
5. My life is not for sale in the mighty name of Jesus.
6. The children that God has ordained for my marriage are not for sale, in the name of Jesus.

7. Every evil seed programmed into the lives of our God ordained children to manifest later in life, be uprooted and die now.

8. Blood of Jesus, buy back .... (Pick from the under listed) if it has been sold off. (Repeat over and over, "Blood of Jesus, buy it back.")

a. my marital destiny   b. my marital joy   c. fulfillment

d. Our peace   e. joy   f. my life   g. Our home

h. my divine partner's life   h. Our children's lives   i. marital blessings

9. Every man or woman from any previous relationship refusing to let me go and fulfill my God ordained marital destiny, release me by fire in the mighty name of Jesus.

10. Blood of Jesus, mercy of God, buy back all of my marital possessions and virtues that witchcraft powers have sold off.

11. Blood of Jesus, mercy of God, buy back all of my divine partner's marital possessions and virtues that witchcraft powers have sold off.

12. Every strongman that has sold off my marriage, your time is up, receive divine judgment, fall down and die now.

13. Every ladder of attack into my life, catch fire and be roasted.

14. Every witchcraft power, personality, or spirit, trading with my marital goodness in any witchcraft market, die.

15. I declare by the power in the blood of Jesus that my God ordained marital home is not for sale, in Jesus name.

16. Every witchcraft bus-stop militating against my marriage, hear the word of the Lord, vomit me now.

17. Every witchcraft bus-stop, hear the word of the Lord, vomit my God ordained spouse.

18. Every evil basket assigned to empty out my marital goodness, catch fire.

19. Every strongman that has sold off my marital goodness, your time is up, somersault and die, in Jesus name.

20. Evil hands assigned against my marriage catch fire, wither, and die.

21. Every power trading with my marital destiny, fall down and die.

EVIL MARKS

"From henceforth let no man trouble me: for I bear in my body the marks of the Lord Jesus." Galatians 6:17.

"And the Lord said unto him, Go through the midst of the city, through the midst of Jerusalem, and set a mark upon the foreheads of the men that sigh and that cry for all the abominations that be done in the midst thereof."
Ezekiel 9:4.

Marks are identification marks that mark you out for good or for evil. From the scriptures above we see that God marks His children for good. For everything that God does, the devil has a counterfeit. So the devil also puts evil marks on people. Witchcraft powers put evil marks on a person spiritually to identify him or her for trouble.

The evil marks attract hatred, problems, and troubles to such a person wherever he or she goes. They bring disfavor and keep the correct suitors away from a person while magnetizing the wrong ones. They also mark a person out for attacks and afflictions such as failure, frustration, rejection, disappointment, bad-luck, tragedy, and satanic oppression.

The blood of Jesus can wash away evil marks and purge away their effect from a person's life. **Revelation 12:11.** You can also ask the Holy Ghost to use the sponge and soap of heaven to give you a divine bath. This will purge and cleanse you of every evil marks and their negative effects upon your life.

DO IT RIGHT THIS TIME

PRAYERS TO ERASE WITCHCRAFT MARKS

Song: There is power, there is power, there is power, in the blood.

1. Blood of Jesus, wipe away every evil mark on my body and spirit.
2. Holy Ghost, use the soap of heaven and sponge of heaven to give me a bath.
3. Holy Ghost wash away every evil mark and handwriting of darkness upon my life, in the name of Jesus.
4. Everything planted in my life to monitor me and mark me out for trouble, catch fire, and die now.
5. Blood of Jesus wipe away every evil writing and label, linking me to any evil association.
6. I cancel the plans and the marks of the enemy upon my life with the blood of Jesus.
7. Marks of rejection, failure, demotion, and disappointment, be erased by the blood of Jesus.
8. Every mark of hatred and disfavor put upon me, be wiped off by the blood of Jesus.
9. Every evil label and satanic hand writings from my foundation, be purged by the blood of Jesus.
10. Every incision and evil deposit in my body dry up, die, and fall away.
11. Every mark of "touch not" keeping my God ordained marital partner away from me be erased by the blood of Jesus.
12. Every power that is secretly oppressing my marital life, be exposed, be disgraced, and die.

DO IT RIGHT THIS TIME

WITCHCRAFT BURIAL (JOHN 11:43-44)

"And when he thus had spoken, he cried with a loud voice, Lazarus, come forth. And he that was dead came forth, bound hand and foot with grave clothes: and his face was bound about with a napkin. Jesus saith unto them, Loose him, and let him go." John 11:43-44.

The Bible verse quoted above describes the burial and resurrection of Lazarus who was a friend of Jesus. Just like Lazarus was buried, witchcraft powers carry out satanic burial of people, things, or places. Various aspects of a person's life can be buried as well. These things that are buried are important things that their victims need to move forward in life and to fulfill their God given destiny. It could be a person's virtues, potentials, marriage, wealth, health, job, business, vehicles, spouses, children, sexual organs, and even academic certificates and other documents of advancement. They are usually buried in the water, earth, trees, forests, witchcraft cauldrons, and other satanic banks. Until these things are spiritually exhumed and resurrected like Lazarus, they are of no use to anyone.

Some people's spouses have been spiritually buried. Until they are exhumed through deliverance and hot prayers just like Jesus exhumed Lazarus, it will be impossible for such people to locate their correct spouses. This is because anything that is satanically buried is no longer available for its divinely ordained purpose until they are spiritually exhumed.

Today, I pray that the power of God will exhume every part of your life and marriage that has been satanically buried.

DO IT RIGHT THIS TIME

PRAYERS TO REVERSE WITCHCRAFT BURIAL

Song: 1. Dry bones must rise again 2. All dry bones you must be revived.

1. Power of God, incubate my life, in the name of Jesus.
2. (Put your right hand on your head and pray this prayer). Resurrection power of our Lord Jesus Christ, fall upon every area of my life. (Mention various areas of your life one by one).
3. By the resurrection power of our Lord Jesus Christ, I disgrace every witchcraft burial conducted for my sake in Jesus name.
4. Blood of Jesus, disgrace every witchcraft burial conducted for the sake of my God ordained spouse.
5. Every witchcraft burial of my marriage, I cancel you by fire.
6. Every good thing that the enemy has buried in my life, come alive and manifest now.
7. Every good thing that is dead in my life, receive new life by fire.
8. Every satanic mortar pounding my marital destiny, catch fire and be roasted.
9. Every evil pot cooking the affairs of my life, shatter and die.
10. You, my buried divine partner, be exhumed and locate me by fire.
11. I ... (mention your name) jump out of every witchcraft grave in the name of Jesus.
12. You my marital destiny buried in the waters, jump out and locate me by fire now.
13. Anything that representing me and my marriage on any evil altar, I separate myself from you now and I set you on fire, be roasted to ashes, in the name of Jesus.
14. Angels of the living God, search through the land of the living and of the dead and retrieve my lost marital glory.
15. Every dead person holding on to my marital goodness, release it, die, and remain dead, in the name of Jesus.
16. I recall and retrieve all my blessings that have been thrown into the water, the forest, and satanic banks, in Jesus name.

107

WITCHCRAFT PLANTATIONS

"But he answered and said, every plant which my heavenly father has not planted shall be rooted up." Matthew 15:13.

Evil plantation is another weapon that witchcraft powers use to harass their victims in the area of marriage. Evil deposits and plantations come into a life through various means such as incisions in the body, tribal marks, tattoos, blood covenants, and ancestral marks. They can be introduced into a life through physically and spiritual means. These include food and drinks taken in the dream and polluted food and drink taken in wrong places in the physical. Another way is through sex in the dream and sex in the physical with demonic partners.

Other sources include urine, excreta, sperm, spit, hot pepper and other terrible things being poured or smeared on people in their dreams. Some people are bitten, cut, slashed, shot or injected in their dreams. Some are fed with all sorts of drinks and food in the dream to weaken them spiritually and to introduce sickness and other problems into their lives. Some engage in sex with people of the opposite or the same sex in the dream. Evil plantations and deposits are left behind from such evil encounters that defile the spirit and the body. Hidden covenants are also formed through them. These all bring problems and afflictions.

Evil plantations can also be introduced into a person's blood and body organs to bring all sorts of terrible diseases into such a life. People have gone to bed healthy only to be injected or given things to eat or drink in their dreams. By the time they woke up they end up with diseases such as cancer, Alzheimer disease, acquired deficiency syndrome (AIDS), leprosy, diabetes, and other debilitating diseases. Some never even wake up but die in their sleep after these terrible dream attacks.

Evil plantations defile a person. God does not want His people polluted:

"You (God) will not allow your holy one to see corruption." Psalm 16:10.

Yet the devil specializes in polluting God's children as noted below:

"But while men slept, his enemy came and sowed tares among the wheat, and went his way." Matthew 13:25.

Spiritual defilement is an evil load that you should get rid of as soon as possible and by all means. This is because God cannot behold corruption so it will separate you from His presence and hinder your prayers

Evil plantations are evil trees that have to be spiritually uprooted because if you just cut it and leave the roots, it will grow again. You have to challenge your spirit, soul, and body with the blood of Jesus and the fire of the Holy Ghost. You should also challenge different areas of your life such as marriage and health with Holy Ghost fire and the blood of Jesus. This is to purge, uproot, and flush out the evil plantation. After doing that then you should pray for restoration of all that they have destroyed in your life. For example, evil plantations from sex in the dream can prevent you from having children. You should therefore first use the fire of God and the blood of Jesus to flush them out. After this you should pray for restoration in various areas including the restoration of your health and the ability to get pregnant and have healthy babies.

PRAYERS TO UPROOT WITCHCRAFT PLANTATIONS AND DEPOSITS

1. Every evil product in my body, be flushed out by the blood of Jesus.
2. O Lord, uproot everything that the enemy has programmed into my marital life to destroy me.
3. Every evil programmer planting evil fruits in the garden of my life and marriage, carry your evil load and go, in the name of Jesus.
4. Evil hands planting evil seeds into my marital destiny in my dream wither and burn to ashes.

5. Every evil thing that I have been fed with in my dream, I vomit you now. Come out with all your roots (stick your fingers in your throat to force it out).

6. Evil hands planting affliction and evil fruits into my marital life, wither and die now.

7 Every power assigned to turn my life upside down, die now.

8. Every evil thing planted in my body to kill me, come out and die, in the name of Jesus.

9. Every witchcraft plantation in my body, come out by fire, be flushed out by the blood of Jesus.

10. Evil incisions in my body, working against my marriage, dry up, fall off, and die, in the name of Jesus.

11. Every good thing the enemy has destroyed in my life, O Lord, restore it by fire.

12. Every good thing stolen from my life in my mother's womb, be restored now, in the name of Jesus.

13. Every evil thing planted in my destiny that is keeping good things away from me, come out with all your roots now and die, in the name of Jesus.

14. Blood of Jesus purge the effect of every demonic access to my blood.

15. I transfuse my blood with the blood of Jesus.

16. I vomit every evil food eaten from the table of the enemy.

17. Satanic caterer assigned against my life, fall down and die.

18. Let all the cooking utensils and equipment of evil caterers be destroyed.

19. Satanic programmers programming evil into my life and marriage, fall down and die.

20. Every evil programmed into my marital life to manifest at a future date, I cancel your maturity date by the blood of Jesus

21. Blood of Jesus, restore all that witchcraft plantations have destroyed in my life and marriage, in the name of Jesus

EVIL GARMENTS (JOSHUA 3:3-4)

We have spiritual garments just like we have the physical garments. A spiritual garment is whatsoever you are wearing in the spiritual realm. It can be good or it can be evil. It can be pure or it can be defiled and polluted. It may be dirty like the dirty garments that Joshua the High Priest wore in the **Zechariah 3:3-4.** They seriously hindered him until the angel changed them to clean garments. Blind Bartimaeus's garments also hindered him, making him a blind beggar. He had to cast them away before he could receive his deliverance, healing, and restoration. **Mark 10:50-52.**

An evil garment is an evil spiritual covering. It manifests in different ways in the physical. Such manifestations include shame, disgrace, embarrassment, blindness, rejection, disappointment, demotion, and other undesirable spirits. It could be disfavor, error, and confusion. For example, if you keep seeing yourself naked in the dream, then you need to pray against the spirit of shame and disgrace. If you see your clothes stained you should deal with the spirit of reproach. If you face rejection often, sometimes even in your dreams, then you should address the spirit of rejection. You should set the garment of rejection ablaze through prayers as rejection will deny you of the good things that are rightfully yours and provoke hatred where there should be favor.

Sometimes these things are hiding in our foundation, just waiting to manifest. They could also be evil carryovers from previous relationships.

Evil garments such as blankets and veils are used to cover up people in the spirit to prevent them from being located by their rightful spouse. Such people waste their time in all the wrong relationships whereas their divinely ordained spouses have been spiritually kidnapped and hidden away under evil blankets. Such garments are also used to cover up people's glory so from shining.

I pray that if you are the victim of evil garments, that the Lord will give you brand new garments today that will move your marital journey forward in Jesus name.

We need divine intervention folks to come out of these situations where the devil has boxed us into a corner. Close your eyes and pray the following prayers aggressively like a wounded lion.

PRAYERS TO DESTROY WITCHCRAFT GARMENTS

Song: Owners of evil load carry your load.

1. Every power sowing evil garments into my marital destiny, fall down and die, in the mighty name of Jesus.
2. My God ordained spouse, wherever you have been hidden to prevent you from finding me, come out and locate me now by fire in the name of Jesus. (Repeat over and over "come out, locate me now.")
3. Every evil garment covering my divine spouse, catch fire and be roasted.
4. Every evil wedding garment preventing me from getting married roast by fire in the name of Jesus.
5. Every strongman keeping my spouse in captivity, I bind you and I command you to release him and let him go.
6. Every evil tree harboring my marital possessions, release them, be uprooted, and be roasted to ashes. (Name the possessions one by one including wedding gown. spouse, marriage, and ring),
7. Every garment of darkness, militating against my marital destiny, catch fire and be roasted to ashes.
8. Every root and seed of nakedness, in my foundation, be uprooted and die.
9. Holy Spirit put me and my God ordained partner on the same page, in the name of Jesus.
10. Blood of Jesus, wash clean every garment stained with sin that is hindering my marriage.
11. Holy Spirit, be my seamstress and sew every rip and every tear on my marital garment.
12. Blood of Jesus, wash away every stain of reproach upon my garment.
13. Blood of Jesus, wash away every stain of reproach upon the garment of my divine partner.
14. I use my garment to wipe away every reproach marring the face of my divine partner.

15. You my flesh, hear the word of the Lord, you will not destroy me, therefore, die now.

16. Every garment of rejection fashioned against me catch fire, be roasted to ashes.

17. I cancel the effect of every dream of nakedness by the power in the blood of Jesus.

18. I reject every garment of the enemy and I return it back to sender.

19. Oh God, arise and intervene speedily in my marital situation today.

20. As you mention the under listed garments, say three times:

"Catch fire, catch fire, catch fire, and be roasted in Jesus name."

a.) Garment of shame

b) Garment of reproach

c) Garment of disfavor

d) Garment of blindness

e) Garment of poverty

f) Garment of slavery

g) Garment of frustration

h) Garment of bad luck

i) Garment of deafness

j) Garment of infirmity

k) Garment of madness

l) Garment of insanity

m) Garment of untimely death

n) Garment of non-achievement

o) Garment of discouragement

p) Garment of loneliness

q) Garment of confusion

r) Garment of nakedness

WITCHCRAFT VERDICTS AND DECREES

"Woe unto them who decree unrighteous decrees, and who write grievousness which they have prescribed." Isaiah 10:1.

Witchcraft verdicts, decrees, and vows are witchcraft decisions taken against a person's life at evil meetings. Close your eyes and pray this prayer:

Every evil meeting arranged for my sake, scatter by thunder, in the name of Jesus.

They are satanic judgments pronounced against a person's life at witchcraft meetings. The verdict could be as simple as "You will never settle down in marriage" or "No man will ever ask for your hand in marriage." It could be a verdict pronounced by a wicked parent or step parent of "All your sisters will marry before you." It could also "You will marry but not enjoy it."

An evil verdict can operate across generational lines until they are properly revoked and reversed. Evil verdicts and decrees should be revoked, reversed, or broken using the blood of Jesus. **Colossians 2:14-15, Galatians 3:13-14.**

PRAYERS TO REVOKE EVIL VERDICTS AND DECREES

1. I refuse to be diverted from my path of marital blessings.
2. Every evil verdict, decree, and judgment over my marital destiny be overturned and reversed.
3. I reject and cancel every evil verdict, decree, and judgment issued against my marital destiny by the blood of Jesus.
4. Every satanic court summoned to deliberate on my marriage, scatter.
5. No evil vow, decision, or prophesy, shall come to pass in my life.

114

6. Father Lord, let every curse of impossibility issued against me backfire to sender in the name of Jesus.

7. Every satanic cobweb assigned to arrest or to divert my marital destiny, catch fire and be roasted to ashes.

8. All powers sponsoring evil decisions and judgments against my marriage, be exposed, be disgraced, and die.

9. All negative words, incantations, and pronouncements uttered by poisonous tongues against my marital success, be completely nullified by the blood of Jesus.

10. Every conspiracy and gang-up against my life and marriage, scatter now.

11. All those who want me out of the way because I am a threat to them be paralyzed by fire.

12. Every personality, spirit, and power saying over their dead body will I marry, it is now time for me to marry, therefore, die now, in the name of Jesus.

13. Every accusing tongue be cut off by fire, in the name of Jesus.

14. Evil voices speaking against my marriage, be silenced by fire.

15. By the power in the blood of Jesus, I refuse to obey any evil command and edict.

16. I turn back from every evil marital journey that I have ever embarked on, in the name of Jesus.

17. I refuse to sit on any evil seat constructed for my by the enemies of my marriage. I set it on fire and command it to burn to ashes.

18. As you mention the under listed evil decrees and verdicts, say three times: "Be reversed and be nullified by the blood of Jesus."

Every evil decree or/and verdict of:

a.) You will never settle down in life   b) You will never marry

c) You will marry but not enjoy it   d) Barrenness

e) You will be jumping from one marriage to another

f) You will never know the joy of parenthood g) Divorce

h) No man will desire you   i) Poverty

j) No woman will marry you   k) insanity

l) Polygamous witchcraft powers   m) Untimely death

DO IT RIGHT THIS TIME

WITCHCRAFT POTS

Witchcraft pots are also known as witchcraft cauldrons. They are used by witchcraft powers to manipulate various areas of their victim's life including marriage. They are also used by witches and wizards to drink the milk of their victim's, life. This means that they eat up the goodness that God has planned for such lives including marital goodness.

Sometimes, these evil pots contain the personal effects of victims which are used to manipulate various areas of their lives including marriage. Such personal effects include placenta, hair, clothes, shoes, and blood. Some witches keep polluted water in their pots which they feed their victims either in the dream or in the physical thereby polluting their lives and marriage. Witchcraft pots are also used to manipulate people's blood, brains and other body organs thereby introducing sickness into the lives of their victims.

PRAYERS TO DESTROY WITCHCRAFT POTS

1. I reject every evil ordination and control.
2. You my life and marriage reject bewitchment.
3. Caldrons assigned against my marital destiny   j, break by fire, in the name of Jesus.
4. Every evil pot harassing my life and marital destiny, I smash you into irreparable pieces.
5. Every power, spirit, and personality manipulating my life and marriage with an evil pot, die with your pot in the name of Jesus.
6. Every power monitoring my life and marriage through an evil pot, fall down and die.
7. Every evil pot controlling my health, and the powers behind it break and die.
8. I release my life and marriage from every evil cauldron by the power in the blood of Jesus.
9. I break the backbone of every evil pot assigned against my life.
10. Blood of Jesus repair every damage that evil cauldrons have done to my marriage.

PLACENTA MANIPULATION (Ezekiel 16:6)

Witchcraft powers often use a person's placenta as a weapon against a person's life. They can be used to manipulate various areas of a person's live including health, finances, and marriage.

It is important to find out how your placenta was disposed of as that might be the cause of your marital woes. The proper way to do this is to burn it. However, many people had their placentas kept in evil pots, buried under evil trees, and in some cases even eaten by wicked authority figures such as grandparents and parents. Various areas of such lives can become unstable as they are manipulated through this demonic access to their placenta. Some placentas are thrown into rivers and other water sources making them easy target for marine witchcraft powers to use to manipulate their victims.

PRAYERS TO OBTAIN DELIVERANCE FROM PLACENTA WITCHCRAFT

1. I reject every evil ordination and control.
2. Every placenta witchcraft targeted against my life and marital destiny, die by fire, in Jesus name.
3. Every chain of darkness around my waist, break, in the name of Jesus. (Lay your hand on your belly-button)
4. Every satanic transfer into my marital destiny through the placenta, I cut you off, in the name of Jesus.
5. Every power utilizing my placenta to summon my spirit, I break your power, in the name of Jesus.
6. Every evil tree manipulating my life and marital destiny, be uprooted and burned to ashes.
7. Every power using my placenta against me, what are you waiting for, fall down and die, in the name of Jesus.
8. By the power in the blood of Jesus I repossess everything that I have lost through placenta witchcraft.

117

MARINE WITCHCRAFT

Marine witchcraft is witchcraft from the waters. There is a marine world under the waters from which marine powers perpetuate terrible witchcraft activities against people, communities, and even countries. **Revelation 12:12**. Marine spirits are extremely stubborn, proud, destructive, and unrepentant spirits from the waters that seek to destroy every facet of their victim's life including marriage.

Marine powers are worshipped in various parts of the world. There are marine priests that maintain marine altars and also initiate covenants between people and these wicked powers. There are marine strongmen that supervise these evil covenants and enforce the negative sanctions that kick in when they are broken. A marine strongman may be a serpent but take on the form of man or woman to sexually violate its victim in the dream.

Victims of marine powers are lured into evil dedication to marine powers in various ways. This could be through partaking in evil spiritual baths in polluted rivers. It could be through ancestral and parental initiations. An evil marine dedication effectively makes a person the property of marine powers. It also marries you off to marine powers such as Queen of the Coast, also known by various other names such as Water mammy, Mammy water, Olokun, and Yemoja. So long as these spiritual marriages are in place, marriage in the physical becomes highly unattainable if not impossible.

The result is satanic delay in getting married or no marriage at all. If you are able to escape from their clutches and get married they ensure that you do not enjoy any moment of the marriage. They cause marital instability by using various weapons against the marriage such as barrenness, miscarriages, abortion of goodness, impotence, sexual intercourse in dreams, low sperm count, and sicknesses such as fibroids and amenorrhea.

There are other open doors through which marine spirits can operate in a person's life. These include evil inheritance; sex with marine agents; evil laying on of hands by demonically possessed priests, pastors, and hair salon attendants; evil covenants; evil parties, attending marine powered churches; ritual baths in polluted rivers and bodies of water; eating polluted food; sharing personal effects with marine agents, using materials from the marine kingdom; and evil sacrifices.

Symptoms indicating that a person's life is under marine harassment include dreams of water; attacks by stubborn and vicious spirit spouses; sex in the dream; seeing or being attacked by marine animals such as crocodiles, water turtles, and serpents; uncontrollable sexual urges; poverty; dream attacks; having spirit children; miscarriages and barrenness; and marital delays and failure.

The way out of this bondage is to break all covenants keeping evil initiations and dedications to marine powers in place. You should renounce and revoke your membership of evil marine societies such as Queen of the Coast and mermaid societies. You also have to pray targeted bombarding prayers against them. You should do spiritual warfare against them daily. You should employ your spiritual weapons to battle them. Some of the most effective weapons to use against them include the name of Jesus, the blood of Jesus, sword of the Lord, lightning, thunder, and tempest of the Lord. And then you have to barricade your life with the fire of the Holy Ghost and the blood of Jesus to prevent any regrouping, counterattacks, and reinforcement.

You should also ensure that you are living a holy life and that you do not have their materials in your possession. These materials include their robes, candles, incense, crosses, creams, soap, and sponge. Endeavor to go for deliverance periodically to ensure that they do not regroup against you. Always rededicate your body, soul, spirit, home, and possessions, to the Father, Son and Holy Spirit every day.

DO IT RIGHT THIS TIME

PRAYERS TO OVERCOME MARINE WITCHCRAFT

1. Every agent of marine witchcraft physically attached to my marital life to frustrate it, die.
2. Every agent of marine witchcraft posing as my husband, wife, parent, or twin, in my dreams, be roasted.
3. Every marine power harassing me in my dreams sexually, I cut off your manhood, womanhood. (Actually demonstrate cutting it off with a sword).
4. My life, refuse every bewitchment, in Jesus name.
5. I destroy the power of any evil transfer from my mother's womb.
6. I break every evil dedication to water spirits and the yokes attached to it, in the name of Jesus.
7. I dismantle and frustrate every marine investment in my life.
8. Every area of cooperation with water spirits in my life, be broken.
9. Fire of God, destroy every mantle of marine and familiar spirit in my life.
10. Every deposit of marine spirit and water spirit in my life, be flushed out by the blood of Jesus.
11. Every covenant with the waters operating in my life, break and die by the power in the blood of Jesus.
12. I renounce and revoke my membership of any marine association (Name them one by one and renounce and revoke them: mermaid society, Queen of the coast society, etc.), in the name of Jesus.
13. By the power in the blood of Jesus, I separate myself from every marine parent. I command him or her to die by fire.
14. I break every curse emanating from broken covenants with marine powers by the blood of Jesus.
15. Let the head of every marine power fashioned against me be smashed to pieces.
16. I break the head of any marine serpent fashioned against me.
17. Every marine power, spirit, or personality hiding in my life to do evil, you are a stranger, come out and die.
18. Marine powered afflictions in my life, die now.

19. Every rage of marine powers targeted against my settling down in marriage, be quenched by the blood of Jesus.

20. Every marine pool separating me from my spouse, dry up.

21. Every marine animal assigned against my marriage, I chain you and return you back to sender.

22. Power of God, destroy every yoke with marine powers operating in my life.

23. Marine Powers Release me and Let me go

24. Stubborn marine spirit husband working against my earthly marriage, you are a liar, die in the name of Jesus.

25. Olokun (River or water mammy) and Mermaid society that has sworn that I will never marry, release me and let me go.

26. You powers from the waters attacking my marital destiny, die, in the name of Jesus.

END OF CHAPTER PRAYERS

1. Where is the Lord God of Elijah? Arise and destroy every power on assignment to destroy my God ordained marriage, in the name of Jesus.

2. You the teeth of the enemy over my marriage, break now.

3. Every power, personality, or spirit that has accepted wickedness and witchcraft to fight my marriage fail and die, in the name of Jesus.

4. Blood of Jesus, remove every unprogressive label from my marital life.

5. Witchcraft sponsored evil marital patterns in my life break.

6. Witches and wizards in charge of my marital problems, lose your hold and die, in the name of Jesus.

7. I pursue, I overtake, and I recover my possessions from witchcraft covens.

8. Every witchcraft power hiding my marital shoes, release them and die.

9. Ever power lighting candles and carrying out rituals against my marriage, die with your candles, in the name of Jesus.

10. Voices of witchcraft speaking against my marital joy, die by fire, in the name of Jesus.

11. Any power, spirit, or personality manipulating me and my divinely ordained partner into wrong relationships to divert our destinies, die, in the name of Jesus.

12. O Lord stretch forth your hand from heaven and remove me and my divine partner from every witchcraft bus-stop.

13. Every witchcraft cage, release me and release my divine partner, in the name of Jesus.

14. I separate myself from every evil tree representing me; harboring my marital virtues; and preventing me from getting married. I uproot it and set it on fire.

15. By the power in the blood of Jesus, I break myself and my God ordained spouse lose from all evil curses, chains, spells, jinxes, bewitchments, witchcraft and sorcery which may have been put on us.

16. Any evil material transferred into my body through contact with any witchcraft agent, roast by fire.

17. Let the effect of any witchcraft summoning of my spirit, be reversed by the blood of Jesus.

18. Witchcraft brooms sweeping away good things from my life, be roasted.

19. Any evil done against my marriage so far through witchcraft oppression and manipulation, be reversed by the blood of Jesus.

20. I fire back every arrow of marital destiny transfer, exchange, and demotion.

21. Every witchcraft exchange of my glory, virtues, and goodness, be reversed by the blood of Jesus.

22. I refuse to be diverted from my God ordained marital destiny.

23. I renounce and break all curses and bewitchment put upon my marital life.

24. Dark veils covering my face, to keep my spouse from locating me, be removed by fire.

25. Any person that is circulating my name to witchcraft covens, die by thunder in the name of Jesus.

26. Light of God, swallow up every darkness that has settled around my marriage.

27. Every chain of darkness binding my hands and feet and preventing my marital life from moving forward, break.

28. Witchcraft chains and ropes assigned against my marriage, catch fire.

29. Every Goliath assigned against my marital elevation and promotion, die.

30. Every evil wind and stone assigned to demote my marital destiny, backfire.

31. Every magnet of darkness pulling the wrong people to me, be roasted.

32. Every power pressing the sand against my marriage, be paralyzed and die.

33. Every trap of witchcraft set for me and my God ordained spouse, catch your owner.

34. Every witchcraft vehicle and driver assigned against my marriage, I separate my life from you and I set you on fire. Burn to ashes.

35. O Lord, restore all the distance that witchcraft powers have stolen from my marital destiny.

36. Every power stealing from the garden of my marital destiny, die, now.

37. O Lord, stretch forth your hand from heaven and place me in the beautiful marital garden that you have prepared for me.

CHAPTER 11

HINDRANCES TO DOING IT RIGHT

There are other factors that can hinder a person from getting married the God ordained way, to the God ordained person, and at the God ordained time besides foundational problems and witchcraft manipulations which were discussed in the last two chapters. These constitute obstacles and embargos that can prevent or at the very least hinder a person from doing it right this time around. They can delay and prevent a person from fulfilling their marital destiny. We should identify these forces and overcome them so that not only will we get married, but our homes will be peaceful and our marriages blissful. In this section, we will identify and address these forces but before we do, let us sing the following warfare song and pray the prayers that follow it militantly:

> **By fire by force I am moving forward**
> **By fire by force**
> **I am moving forward**
> **By fire by force I am moving forward**
> **I am moving forward**
> *(Repeat this last line several times and demonstrate it by*
> *actually moving forward physically).*

PRAYERS

1. **O Lord, arise by all the powers by which you are known as God and move my marital life forward by fire, in the name of Jesus.**
2. **Marital bliss, my life is available. Locate me by fire, in the mighty name of Jesus.**

124

3. I put on my feet the supernatural shoes of Jesus. I shall not fail and I shall not fall in marriage, in the name of Jesus.

1. DISOBEDIENCE AND SIN

"To obey is better than sacrifice. (1 Samuel 15:22).

"If ye be willing and obedient, ye shall eat the good of the land." Isaiah 1:19.

Willingness and obedience makes us to eat the good of the land. It is when we are obedient that God will bless us. On the other hand, disobedience and sin bring down God's wrath which can jeopardize breakthroughs in every area of our lives, including marriage.

"If ye be willing and obedient, ye shall eat the good of the land: But if ye refuse and rebel, ye shall be devoured with the sword: for the mouth of the Lord hath spoken it." Isaiah 1:19-20.

We should not ever argue with God. Instead we should pull down everything in our lives that wants to stand against God and His counsel.

"Casting down imaginations, and every high thing that exalteth itself against the knowledge of God, and bringing into captivity every thought to the obedience of Christ; And having in a readiness to revenge all disobedience, when your obedience is fulfilled." 2 Corinthians 10:6-7.

God knows the beginning and the end of every matter. He can see through people's motives, deceptions, and ploys. Samson, one of leaders of Israel, had to learn this lesson the hard way. God sent an angel to announce his birth and ordained a glorious destiny for him but Samson destroyed it with his own hands. In rebellion, he refused to take the godly counsel of parents not to be unequally yoked in marriage to a non-Jew. **Judges 14:1-3**. In the process he disobeyed God's laws that forbade Jews from marrying non-Jews and lived to regret it. His wife sold him out to his enemies, the Philistines, who plucked out his eyes and put him to hard labor. He died while in their custody. **Judges 16:20-31.** His was a classic illustration of the scripture that says that there is a way that seems right to a man but the end is death. **Proverb 14:12.**

2. FEAR

"For God hath not given us the spirit of fear but of love, of power and of a sound mind." 1Timothy 1:7.

Fear is not of God but of the devil. It brings torment into a person's life. **1 John 4:18.** Faith on the other hands is the opposite of fear. It brings confidence and trust in God. Faith says "I can do all things through Christ that strengthens me," whereas fear says "I am too old, no man could possibly want to marry me now". Fear says "I have reached menopause, I could never have a baby now." Faith says "I will bring forth fruits in my old age."

Faith is the currency of Heaven. We use our faith to turn God's promises for our lives into reality. Faith comes from internalizing the word of God. **Romans 10:17.** Everyone is responsible for developing their own faith hence God blesses everyone according to his faith. **Matthew 9:29.** Abraham stands out in the Bible as the father of faith. The Bible describes his faith in the following passage:

"*And being not weak in faith*, he considered not his own body now dead, when he was about an hundred years old, neither yet the deadness of Sarah's womb: *He staggered not at the promise of God through unbelief; but was strong in faith, giving glory to God;* And being fully persuaded that, what he had promised, he was able also to perform. And therefore it was imputed to him for righteousness. *Now it was not written for his sake alone, that it was imputed to him; But for us also, to whom it shall be imputed,* if we believe on him that raised up Jesus our Lord from the dead; Who was delivered for our offences, and was raised again for our justification." Romans 4:19-25.

126

From the above passage, we see that we should not allow fear into our heart as it can abort the new things that God wants to do in our lives. Moreover, we are Abraham's children through Christ so we should emulate him and be people of faith. We have to trust God and believe that He rewards all who diligently seek Him. **Hebrews 11:6.** Now close your eyes and pray this prayer:

I bind and cast out every spirit of fear denying me of my marital breakthrough, in the mighty name of Jesus.

3. DISCOURAGEMENT AND FRUSTRATION

This is another weapon that the enemy uses to attack our peace and faith in God's word concerning our marital situation. The devil brings frustration and discouragement to make us think that there is no way out for us out being single. He convinces us that because we have had bad relationships in the past, we can never have good marriages. Discouragement opens the door for the devil to come in and steal good things from us. It turns winners into losers.

King David gave us the key for dealing with discouragement. We are told that David and his men got home and meet that their families had been abducted and taken captive. The people around him were so discouraged that they wanted to stone him. The Bible records that David, however, encouraged himself in the Lord. **1 Samuel 30:4-6.** Not only that, he had victory at last.

We too can encourage ourselves in the Lord by fighting back with the word of God, praises, worship, prayers, and fellowship with other believers. **Ephesians 5:19; Colossians 3:16.** No matter how bad the outlook, discouragement will not be able to cripple us if we remain in the Lord's presence and in the midst of His people. We can also sing to the situation.

Singing songs of encouragement and hope will discomfit the powers behind discouragement and frustration in our lives. It will also encourage us and give us hope. Below is one of my favorites:

God will make a way
Where there seems to be no way
He works in ways we cannot see
He will make a way for me
He will be my guide
Draw me closely to His side
With love and strength
For each new day
God will make a way
God will make a way

I know that it might not look or feel like God can make a way right now. But even this singlehood, spinsterhood, bachelorhood, lateness in marriage, mockery, loneliness, and other marital challenges that you are facing shall pass. In the end, God will meet you at your point of need and make a way for you. Everyone around you shall see it and rejoice with you in Jesus name. Amen!!!!

4. REJECTION, DISAPPOINTMENT, AND FAILURE

Please, take these prayers with me:

1. Every power assigned to turn my glory to shame, die now, in the name of Jesus
2. Evil arrow, fired into my life by day and by night, come out and backfire, in the mighty name of Jesus.
3. Every arrow of rejection fired against my marriage, I fire you back.

Many who are trying to get married in a godly way, are battling the spirit of rejection, disappoint, and failure at one level or the other. Today, our encouragement should come from the word of God which tells us that we are no longer rejected but are accepted in Christ Jesus, the Beloved.

128

"To the praise of the glory of his grace, wherein he hath made us accepted in the beloved." Ephesians 1:6.

Rejection is a spirit that often creeps in through the back door through such avenues as disappointments suffered in previous relationships. Sometimes, it has its roots in a person's foundation. It is an evil seed, root, and tree that has to be uprooted for such a person's destiny to thrive.

Rejection goes hand in hand with self-condemnation which is why the Bible emphasizes that there is no condemnation to those who are in Christ Jesus that walk in the spirit and not the flesh. **Romans 8:1.**

Sometimes rejection, disappointment, failure, and other negative emotions originate from arrows that have been fired into a person by demonic powers and close enemies. The arrows are targeted to confuse; stagnate; slow down; or kill destinies. We must not allow them to remain in our lives. They should be dealt with as a matter of urgency. They are evil load that should be extracted and returned to their senders through violent prayers and deliverance. If this is not done they can create a lot of problems and can even lead to untimely death. You can use the prayers at the end of this section to send them back to the sender.

We also have to be very cautious in picking the people that we associate with. Some time ago a man who paraded himself as "pastor" and whom I met through some "Christian" friends approached me for marriage. I told him that I would seek the Lord's face. Good thing I did because he turned out to be not only a fraud but also highly demonic. During a deliverance program, the so called "pastor" appeared to me in a dream and told me that he poses as a pastor to deceive people. He said that he was actually a witchdoctor and had acquired the demonic power from his father, who was also a witchdoctor. The shocking part was that he said that he put a spell on me to drive away intending suitors from me. He said that he prepared it with chicken feces and that its assignment was to make me to smell like fowl feces whenever a suitor came near me so that he would be repelled and run away.

What gross wickedness! Yet this man and the person that introduced him to me were "ordained pastors." Yet, he sent arrows of rejection and disappointment into my marital destiny. Thank God for sweet Jesus and the provision that He has made for our deliverance and restoration. Thank God also for divine revelation. Sending the arrows back was the easy part. Halleluiah! Praise the Lord. He is worthy!!!

Arrows of rejection can also work by altering a person's physical looks particularly whenever prospective suitors show interest. The person may start looking much older than his or her actual age or they may break out in terrible blemishes, pimples, and boils on their faces making them look very unattractive. These are classic manipulations to delay and prevent marriage by ensuring that no suitor comes and stays.

So we see that arrows can be sent into people's lives to destabilize and hinder them from getting married, or to prevent them from marrying the right person, or marrying at the God appointed time. Once again, it is important that we extract them and return them back to sender through prayers and deliverance. We also should be very careful of our associations and should present all proposals for any marital relationship to God first in prayers for approval before proceeding further.

PRAYERS TO CANCEL THE SPIRIT OF REJECTION

Song: There is power mighty in the blood

1. **Blood of Jesus, wash away every mark, symbol, and handwriting of rejection put upon me from when I was a baby.**
2. **Every seed and root of rejection in my foundation bringing disfavor, hatred, and rejection, be uprooted and die now.**
3. **Everything done under demonic anointing that is keeping the opposite sex away from me, be reversed by the blood of Jesus and let the effect go back to sender. Everything done with (pick from the under listed)..............be reversed by the blood of Jesus.**
 (a) **Evil smell** (b) **Animal or human excreta**
 (c) **Urine** (d) **Demonic alteration of appearance** (e) **incisions and tattoos** (f) **Personal effects (such as hair, shoes, picture, and undies)** (g) **Evil marks, labels, and seals** (h) **images (molded or carved).**

4. Every power sowing the garment of rejection into my destiny, your time is up, die, in Jesus name.

5. Every owner of evil load of rejection, appear now, carry your load and go, in the name of Jesus.

6. Spirit of rejection, I am not your candidate, therefore lose your hold, die, in the name of Jesus

7. Every evil smell from whatsoever source in my life repelling and driving away my God ordained spouse, be replaced with the fragrance of Jesus, the Rose of Sharon, in Jesus' name.

8. Every arrow of rejection fired into my life and marriage, jump out and backfire, in the name of Jesus.

9. Lord, arise and recover for me all that I have lost as a result of rejection, in the name of Jesus.

5. ERRORS AND MISTAKES

These are spirits that cause people to make very expensive mistakes in life that can truncate their marital destiny. Arrows can be sent into people's lives to cause them to make errors by manipulating them into marrying the wrong people while pushing away the right ones. Even when they are given godly counsel they refuse to listen. These mistakes can set a person back several years and it can take years to recover. Some people never even recover from them as it mars their whole life. A good example is the case of Samson whose life was wasted because of his involvement in wrong marital relationships.

We must guard against these spirits in the area of marriage because a mistake in this area is tantamount to destiny wastage as marriage affects all other areas of a person's life. Not only that. It will also affect the destinies of the children born from the marriage and their descendants.

PRAYERS FOR SPIRIT OF ERROR AND MISTAKE

1. If I have taken any wrong road on my marital journey, I turn back now, I retrace my steps.

2. Every arrow of error and mistake, come out and backfire.

3. I recover myself back from every unprofitable journey that I have ever undertaken on my marital life.

4. By the power of the Holy Spirit, I jump off every vehicle that is heading for trouble and disaster matrimonially, in the name of Jesus.

5. Every misleading demon confusing my life, get out now.

6. You spirit of error and mistake I am not your candidate, therefore die by fire, in the name of Jesus.

7. Arrows of destiny wastage jump out and backfire.

8. Every curse promoting error and mistake in my life, break by the blood of Jesus.

9. Powers assigned to divert my marital destiny, fall down and die.

10. Light of God, drive away any darkness that has settled around my marital destiny.

PRAYERS TO RETURN EVIL ARROWS BACK TO SENDER

Let us take this prayer song with great aggression and then follow it up with the prayers that follow.

> Evil arrow
> Go back to your sender
> Evil arrow
> Go back to your sender
> (Repeat the chorus over and over again)

1. I fire back every evil arrow assigned against my marital life.

2. Every seed and root of rejection in my foundation, be uprooted by fire.

3. Owner of evil load affecting my marital destiny I summon you here. Now carry your load, and go.

4. Arrows of ………….. (Mention the under listed) jump out and die in Jesus name.

a) Confusion b) Error c) Mistake d) Rejection
e) Disappointment f) Discouragement g) Demotion
h) Slow progress i) Satanic delay k) reproach

5. Arrows of loneliness and ancestral loneliness, jump out of my life and die.

6. I fire back every arrow of shame and disgrace, in the name of Jesus.

7. Satanic arrows fired into my brain, to terminate my marital destiny, come out and die now.

8. Every arrow of limitation preventing me from moving to my marital next level, scatter and die.

9. Every arrow of stagnancy and backwardness fired into my marital life, come out and backfire.

10. Evil arrows fired to destabilize and hinder my marital life backfire.

6. HOPELESSNESS

"It is good that a man should both hope and quietly wait for the salvation of the Lord." Lamentation 3:26.

The Bible says that hope deferred makes the heart sick. **Proverbs 13:12.** But as Christians we should not allow hopelessness to mar our marital horizon. This is because we have hope that our marital tomorrow will be better than our today because we know that Jesus is in it and with Him by our side we can face anything that the future brings and come out victorious. We should instead emulate Abraham who kept hope alive for twenty five years while waiting for his son Isaac, the son that God had promised him to be born. The Bible says concerning him:

"Who against hope believed in hope, that he might become the father of many nations, according to that which was spoken, so shall thy seed be." Roman 4:18.

What has God promised you in the area of marriage? Hold on to it. Remember it is darkest before the dawn. Do not give up. You victory is just around the corner.

7. EVIL COVENANTS

Covenants are agreement or contracts between two or more people. They usually have inbuilt sanctions that kick in if the terms of the agreement are broken. **2 Samuel 21:1-9.** In the area of marriage, the sanctions may be no marriage, late marriage, sickness, barrenness, insanity, or even untimely death.

There are conscious and unconscious covenants. The sad thing is that even if you do not know that these evil covenants exist, they are still binding on you and can affect your ability to get married successfully. There are evil authorities and powers that supervise these covenants and ensure that their terms are adhered to. For example, there are ancestral strongmen that ensure that the evil contracts in a family are enforced from generation to generation. So you find families where all the females have been married off to evil powers such as marine powers, snakes, lizards, the father of the house, and so on. In others, the strongman of the family has covenanted family members to witchcraft or marine powers. If you are married to a lizard or a snake in the spirit, needless to say no one will come near you in the physical for marriage until that spiritual marriage is nullified through the right kind of prayers and deliverance.

There are some highly demonic covenants that need special mentioning here. One of these is blood covenant. Any kind of agreement backed by blood is very difficult to break and needs special deliverance. Therefore, you should see a trained deliverance minister for urgent attention. **(See details on how to do this in the appendix at the end of the book).** In this category, are couples that have mixed their blood to form covenants in their marital relationships. It is even worse if such a relationship failed and they later marry or try to marry other people.

An evil soul tie is another type of covenant that has serious adverse effects on the ability to get married successfully. It is when a soul is knitted to that of another person or being in a manner that would not bring glory and honor to God. You can break evil soul ties and set yourself free by praying the special prayers at the end of this section. You

134

should mention the name of each person that you have related to in an ungodly manner one by one and break evil soul ties with each one. This includes former or current sexual partners, ex-spouses, friends, bosses, and people that have or have had spiritual authority over you such as pastors and parents.

The good news is that no matter how strong and stubborn a covenant is or how long it has been in place, we can always stand on completed work of our Lord Jesus Christ on the Cross of Calvary and use the scripture verse below to break it:

"Blotting out the handwriting of ordinances that was against us, which was contrary to us, and took it out of the way, nailing it to his cross." Colossians 2:14.

PRAYERS TO BREAK EVIL COVENANTS
(Includes prayers for breaking evil soul ties)

Song: 1. Power in the blood. 2. There is power mighty in blood.

1. I break and loose myself from every evil covenant, in Jesus name.
2. I break and loose myself from every covenanted curse.
3. I renounce all hidden evil soul ties, in the name of Jesus.
4. All evil soul ties with anyone living or dead, break and release me.
5. I break every evil soul tie with ....in the name of Jesus.
(Carry out *this exercise diligently and thoroughly. Write down the names of anyone that you have ever related to in an ungodly manner. Then break any evil soul tie with each person, animal, being, or organization one by one. Do not lump them together. Also get rid of anything keeping the evil soul tie in place such as gifts from former lovers, boyfriends, girlfriend, and sugar daddies.)*
6. Covenants and curses, working against my marital victory and fulfillment, break and die.
7. Every covenant of late marriage, break in the name of Jesus.
8. Every covenant of no marriage, break and die.

9. Every covenant with death that I have made or that anyone has made on my behalf, be annulled by the blood of Jesus.

10.   a. Every strongman supervising covenanted curses that are delaying my marriage, I bind you, in the name of Jesus.

    b. Now, release my marriage and die, in Jesus name.

11. Ancestral covenants misdirecting my marital destiny break by fire.

12. Every power blocking my full scale laughter, fall down and die.

13. Marine sponsored covenants and curses operating in my life and marital destiny, break by the blood of Jesus.

14. Household wickedness sponsored covenants and curses delaying my marital breakthrough, break and release me now.

14. As you mention the various items listed below, you say three hot times: "Break, Break, break, and release me, in the name of Jesus."

a) Every covenant with marine powers. (b) Every evil soul tie and covenant with family and village idols. (c) Every evil soul tie with any dead person. d) Every soul tie and covenant with ancestral powers. e) Every covenant with the water deities.

(f) Every covenant of profitless hard-work.

(g) Covenant with the dead. (h) Covenant with loneliness.

(i) Spiritual marriage (j) Covenant of untimely death.

(k) Every evil soul tie and covenant with any spirit spouse.

(l) Covenants limiting my life (m) Satanic embargos.

(n) Covenant keeping insanity in place.

(o) Covenant of failure at the edge of success.

(p) Evil soul ties (q) Covenant of non-achievement. (r) Covenant of bad luck.

15. Every evil ladder keeping evil covenants in place in my life catch fire, roast.

16. Every evil umbilical cord through which evil is flowing into my life, dry up by fire.

8. UNBROKEN CURSES

Unbroken curses form the root of many problems in people's lives. A curse is anything that is the opposite of a blessing. It can separate you from your marital breakthroughs and success. **Deuteronomy 27:12-13.** Curses are negative words that are spoken into a life, a place, or a thing, with the intention of causing harm and bringing about evil. Curses are not just empty words. They are backed up by demonic power and authority and so should be taken very seriously. Examples of curses are demonic prayers, incantations, spells, and covenanted curses.

The Bible teaches us that every curse has a cause. **Proverb 26:2.** All over the Bible we see the terrible consequences of curses on the lives of people, places, and things. In **2 Kings 5:26-27,** the prophet Elisha put a curse of leprosy on his covetous servant, Gehazi. **2 Kings 5:27.** In **Joshua 6:26,** Joshua the servant of God destroyed the city of Jericho and put a curse on anyone that would rebuild it. He also put a curse of death on the first and last born sons of the person. In **Mark 21:19-21,** Jesus cursed the fig tree and it withered right away to the amazement of those present.

Curses provide legal ground for the devil to deal with a person. It opens the door for them to operate and acts as a ladder for them to climb in carry out evil. They abort or delay good things. They cause automatic failure where there should be success. They invite trouble and usher in hatred, disfavor, bad luck, stagnancy, backwardness, demotion, tragedy, untimely death, and other negative occurrences into people's lives. In the area of marriage, they also magnetize the wrong people to a person and keep the right people away. They frustrate and discourage.

Curses can control a person's life and manipulate such a life out of God's plans and purposes. They target different areas of a person's life including marriage. Such curses include the curse of infirmity, failure, poverty, bad marriage, no marriage, delayed marriage, backwardness, barrenness, bad luck, stagnancy, non-achievement, vagabond lifestyle, demotion, and untimely death. Such curses will need to be broken and such lives realign with God's agenda. Unbroken curses can also affect the offspring of a marriage. For example, Gehazi's descendants were cursed.

137

There could be a curse of profitless hard work which manifests in a person planting and another reaping the fruits of his labor. It also manifests in a person building and another inhabiting. **Isaiah 65:21-23.** For example, you could spend all your time polishing up a young man and sowing into his life hours in prayers, fasting, and encouragement. You do all these believing that he is your God ordained partner and then just when the prayers start to pay off and doors start to open for him he marries someone else. It could be that a man puts a woman through college for the same reason. Then as soon as she graduates she marries someone else. That will not be our portion this time around in Jesus name. Please pray the following prayer with holy madness.

Every curse of profitless hard work operating in my life and marital destiny, break and die by the power in the blood of Jesus.

Curses originate from various sources and remain in operation until properly broken. A curse can kick into a person's life is when the person breaks the terms of a covenant. Curses remain in effect from generation to generation when left unbroken so a person's descendants will be affected as well. A good example is the case of King's Saul's descendants in the Bible. During the time of Joshua, the Israelites made a covenant with the Gibeonites to protect them. Several generations later, King Saul broke the terms of the covenant by slaughtering the Gibeonites. This brought a curse on Israel that manifested in a three year famine in the land. King David prayed to find out the cause of the famine and how to end it. He was asked to hand over Saul's descendants to the Gibeonites. The curse was only broken and the famine came to an end only after the Gibeonites slaughtered Saul's descendants. So we see that the curse kicked in with Saul's action but it was his innocent children paid the price. We also notice that the curse was only broken after David took steps to stop it.

Curses can also originate from one's ancestors like the curse of servitude that Noah put on his son Ham and his descendants. **Genesis 9:24-27.** The case with King Saul and his descendants above is also a good illustration.

Curses can be from evil people in your environment such as where you live, work, school, and even worship. They may originate from jilted or wicked ex-lovers and envious unfriendly friends. They may also come from wicked spiritual authority figures such as wicked parents, bosses, and pastors. Gehazi, in the Bible was cursed by his master, the prophet Elisha. So were his children. **2 Kings 5:26-27.**

A curse can be from God as a consequence of our actions such as rebellion and disobedience to God. For example, worshipping idols brings a curse. So does failure to pay tithe. **Malachi 3:8-13.** The priest Eli and his sons, were cursed because he failed to call his children to order when they abused their office as priests. **1 Samuel 2:27-36.** Anyone that fails to honor their parents is cursed with untimely death. **Exodus 20:12; Ephesians 6:2.**

What is the way out of a cursed life? A curse is not supposed to be able to operate upon a child of God. But if it does, then we should first pray a prayer of repentance for ourselves and for any sin committed by our ancestors. We can use the blood of Jesus to wash away these sins. Then we should inquire from God through prayers the cause of the curse and how to end it like David did when there was a famine. **2 Samuel 21:1.**

Repentance is the solution when a curse is from God from breaking His laws. Other types of curses should be broken from the source using the potent blood of Jesus which was shed for us on Calvary. This is what the prophet Elisha did to clean up cursed Jericho. **2 Kings 2:21.** Moreover, the word of God has made provision for our deliverance from every curse through the finished work of Calvary. Jesus' shed blood is the solution to every curse because He took our place and became a curse for us by hanging on the Cross so we do not have to labor under any curse:

"Christ hath redeemed us from the curse of the law, being made a curse for us: for it is written, Cursed is every one that hangeth on a tree." Galatians 3:13.

Therefore, we can appropriate the blood that He shed on the Cross to break every curse troubling our destinies. I say every curse preventing or delaying our marriage is broken today by the blood of Jesus. We are marching forward to possess our possession in Jesus name.

PRAYERS TO BREAK STUBBORN CURSES

1. Ask God to forgive you for any sin that has allowed curses to thrive in your life.

2. Repent of the sins of your ancestors. Use the blood of Jesus to separate yourself from the sins of your ancestors.

3. Every curse from my foundation preventing me from getting married break in the name of Jesus.

4. Inherited curses troubling my marital star, break.

5. Every curse of late marriage issued against my head, break.

6. Every curse of "You shall not settle down in life," break.

7. Every curse of wrong marriage, break and release me now.

8. Every curse of "No man will marry you," break and die.

9. Every curse controlling my marital destiny, break and die.

10. Anti-marriage curse issued against me, break and die.

11. Every stubborn curse chasing away my divine partner, break by the blood of Jesus.

12. Stubborn covenants and curses causing satanic delay of my marriage, break and die.

13. Every curse of marital failure, break and release me.

14. Evil verdicts working against my getting married, be overturned by the blood of Jesus.

15. Any power that wants to cut off my star, fall down and die.

16. Curses and covenants that have introduced stagnancy into my life, break and release me by fire, in the name of Jesus.

17. Powers keeping stubborn curses that are working against my marriage in place die, in Jesus name.

18. Mention the items listed below and then say three times: "Break, break, break, by the blood of Jesus."

Curses issued by:

a) Parental
b) Environmental powers
c) Jilted lovers
d) Ex-spouses
e) Ancestral curses
f) Witchcraft powers
g) Collective captivity powers
h) Marine powers
i) Polygamous witchcraft
j) Ex boyfriends and girl friends

140

k) Evil authorities   l) Spirit spouses

m) Envious friends   n) unfriendly friends

o) Wicked pastors, prophets, and others with spiritual authority

p) Curse issued by evil competitors

9. BREAKING VOWS AND COVENANTS MADE WITH GOD

As far as God and His word is concerned, a covenant is a covenant, is a covenant! One of the greatest attributes of God that runs through the Bible is that God is the covenant keeping God. **Hebrew 6:13-18.** He expects no less from us. We should willingly keep all the covenants that we have made with God involving any issue in life, including the area of marriage. They are binding contracts, that if not kept can affect every area of our lives and even the destiny of our children yet unborn.

A good example is any vow that we make to God. The Bible warns that it is better not to make such vows than to make them and not fulfill then. **Ecclesiastes 5:4-5.** For example, you should not promise God that you will live a celibate life if you know that you will not keep the vow.

When I first got born again, the Ancient of Days appeared to me in a dream and told me that it is better not to make a vow than to make it and not keep it. It was much later that I found out that what He told me was written in the Bible. It clearly says:

"When thou vowest a vow unto God, defer not to pay it; for he hath no pleasure in fools: pay that which thou hast vowed. Better is it that thou shouldest not vow, than that thou shouldest vow and not pay." Ecclesiastes 5:4-5.

If you have made any vows to God and His servants, please hurry to redeem them. Failure to do so will affect you aversely. Keep your end of all promises made to God and covenants cut with Him and the ever faithful God will keep His own end of the bargain. **Genesis 28:20; Genesis 31:13.**

10. PREJUDICES

Prejudices can deny you of God's best for you in marriage. This is regardless of whether they are based on race, class, income, or education. Racial bias may be based on family, tribe, race, nationality, and color. Scriptures clearly teach us that there is neither Jew nor Greek in the body of Christ. **Galatians 3:28.** We are all His children and the blood of Jesus cleanses and knits us closer than any earthly blood ties ever could. Jesus, when told that His earthly family members were looking for Him, seized the opportunity to teach on who the members of a Christian's family really are. He said they consist of those who know the will of God and do it. **Matthew 12:50.** This tells us that we should be more interested in marrying a God fearing, fired up child of God than some unbeliever recommended by our unsaved and spiritually ignorant family members.

Therefore, you should be aware that prejudices, including those mentioned above, can divert your destiny. It can make you to reject your God ordained spouse and settle for the wrong person, a decision that you will live to regret. Please make the following confessions from your heart:

1. I refuse to cooperate with demotion.
2. I will not marry my enemy.
3. I refuse to close the door of marriage against my own self.

11. IMMORALITY

Immorality includes any kind of sex outside of marriage, such as fornication and adultery. It also includes all types of sexual perversion such as homosexuality, lesbianism, masturbation, oral and anal sex, bestiality, and all other deviant sexual behavior. Engaging in any of these activities defiles and pollutes your life in general and your marital destiny in particular. It also puts you in bad standing before God; bans you from heaven; and makes you a candidate of hell fire as the following scripture shows:

"But outside are dogs and sorcerers, and sexually immoral and murderers and idolaters, and whoever loves and practices a lie." Revelation 22:15.

Above all, it constitutes a very terrible foundation on which to build any kind of marital relationship. Even if such a relationship ends up in marriage, the marriage is already polluted. This will provide a legal door for the devil to come in later and create havoc in the marriage.

If you are in an immoral relationship, you should flee from it now. This is regardless of whether there are children born into the relationship. At the very least you should go through a period of separation, sober reflection, repentance (before God and man), counseling, and deliverance. After that, you should seek God's face through prayers to know His will for you in marriage. It is only if the Lord confirms your former sin partner as His actual choice for you that you can repair the relationship and then proceed in the godly way of getting married this time around as clearly explained in this book.

If the Lord says that your relationship is a mistake and that He has not ordained both of you to marry, please do not push ahead with the relationship even if you have children together. You should go your separate ways and trust God to heal you and bring you His own ordained spouse for you. If you go ahead, a life time of pain, misery, frustration, and lack of fulfillment awaits you. The effect will spill over to your children also.

DO IT RIGHT THIS TIME

You must flee immorality today. You should discipline yourselves by keeping your flesh under. **1 Corinthians 9:27.** By God's grace, we shall all make heaven in Jesus name.

PRAYERS OF DELIVERANCE FROM FORNICATION AND PERVERSION

1. Every inherited demon of sexual perversion in my life, receive the arrows of fire, in the name of Jesus.
2. I command every power of sexual perversion to come against itself, in the name of Jesus.
3. Father Lord, let every demonic stronghold built in my life by the spirit of sexual perversion be pulled down, in the name of Jesus.
4. Let every power of sexual perversion that has consumed my life be shattered to pieces, in the name of Jesus.
5. Let my soul be delivered from the force of sexual perversion, in the name of Jesus
6. Let the Lord God of Elijah, arise with a strong hand against every spirit wife/husband and all the powers of sexual perversion troubling my life, in the name of Jesus.
7. I break the hold of any evil power over my life, in the name of Jesus.
8. I nullify every effect of the bite of sexual perversion upon my life with the blood of Jesus, in the name of Jesus.
9. Every evil stranger and all satanic deposits in my life, I command you to be paralyzed and to get out of my life, in the name of Jesus.
10. Holy Ghost fire, purge my life completely, in the name of Jesus.
11. I claim my complete deliverance from the spirit of fornication and sexual immorality, in the name of Jesus.
12. Let my eyes be delivered from lust, in the name of Jesus.
13. As from today let my eyes be controlled by the Holy Spirit, in the name of Jesus.
14. Holy Ghost fire, fall upon my eyes burn to ashes every evil force and all satanic power controlling my eyes, in the name of Jesus.
15. I move from bondage to liberty in every area of my life, in the name of Jesus.

12. SELFISHNESS, GREED, COVETOUSNESS

We should be accommodating and not expect our God ordained spouse to be perfect or we may be waiting forever. After all, none of us are perfect. Even if we did get our "perfect" person, she may end up being a Delilah that truncates our destiny like Delilah did to Samson's. That "perfect" man may end up being a fire extinguisher, with no interest in the things of God, who puts out your spiritual fire. He may end up destroying your relationship with God; your calling; and even your very life. History is full of men, like Samson, that insisted against all advice on marrying "Delilahs" and ended up paying with their very lives. Others married "Jezebels" who bewitched them, turned them into wimps, and wasted their potentials. .

You should measure your God ordained partner by the standard of the word of God which truly reflects how God sees him or her and not your own carnal selfish standards. You should also stop comparing your partner with others as the Bible says that it is unwise to do so.

"For we dare not make ourselves of the number, or compare ourselves with some that commend themselves: but they measuring themselves by themselves, and comparing themselves among themselves, are not wise." 2 Corinthians 10:12.

Also, we should be willing to give of ourselves and not just be at the receiving end all the time. The key to being blessed is in giving and not in receiving. **Acts 20:35.**

13. PRAYERLESSNESS

"Ye ask, and receive not, because ye ask amiss, that ye may consume it upon your lusts." James 4:3.

The Bible encourages us to always watch and pray. **Ephesians 6:18.** It also admonishes us to be sober and vigilant because the enemy is looking around for whom to devour. **1 Peter 4:7.** Prayerlessness goes beyond not watching, fasting, and praying. It is also when you pray in such a way that the prayers are ineffective.

"The effectual fervent prayer of a righteous man availeth much." James 5:16.

It is like you visiting a doctor who gives you a prescription for three different medicines. The first medicine you are to take one dose three times a day for 3 days. The second, you are to take once a day for 21 days, without missing days. The third medicine, you are to take at exactly 12 mid night every day for 7 days. All three medications have to be taken as prescribed for them to be effective in solving the problems they were prescribed for. It is the same thing with prayers.

For prayers to work, you have to pray them in a certain way and at certain times. We call these targeted prayers. For example, to get victory over household witchcraft, you have to bombard the enemy with prayers over an extended time. These prayers will also be more effective if they are done at night which is when witches hold meetings in their covens to perpetuate evil. It makes no sense for you to be sleeping while they are busy sharing and eating up your organs or transferring your God ordained husband to your best friend. You should battle them between the hours of 12 midnight and 3 a.m.

Our Lord Jesus while teaching on this topic said that for certain prayers to be effective, they have to be accompanied by fasting. **Mark 9:29.** The Bible also talks about the "effectual fervent prayers of a righteous man." **James 5:16.** This means that just like you have effective prayers, you also have ineffective one. For example, according to the passage referenced above, prayers that are prayed by

146

the unrighteous such as wicked people will not be answered. In fact they are an abomination to God. **Proverb 15:8, 29.**

I pray that from now on every prayer that we pray concerning our marriage will be fervent and effective in the name of Jesus. Our prayer arrows will no longer miss their intended targets in Jesus name.

PRAYERS FOR FERVENCY IN PRAYERS

1. O Lord plug me to the socket of your power.
2. My inner man receive fire.
3. Holy Ghost fire, incubate my life.
4. O Lord pour your fire of revival upon my life.
5. O Lord ignite my prayer life by your fire.
6. Fervency in the place of prayer, fall upon my life in a new and dynamic way in the name of Jesus.
7. Every power assigned to douse my prayer fire, you have failed, fall down and die in the name of Jesus.
8. Holy Ghost fire, incubate my spirit-man with Your revival spirit, in the name of Jesus.
9. Let my inner man receive the fire of God to move forward, in the name of Jesus.
10. Let the effect of every dream attack assigned to weaken my prayer life be reversed in the name of Jesus.
11. You spirit of slumber and deep evil sleep I bind you and cast you out of my life.
12. I bind ever spirit of distraction at the place of prayer.

14. UNBELIEF AND DOUBT

"Believe in the Lord your God, so shall ye be established; believe his prophets, so shall ye prosper." 2 Chronicles 20:20.

Unbelief means lack of faith in God and His word. It is failure to trust God and believe His promises to you. This includes promises from the Bible and His rhema word to you specifically. God hates unbelief and it can have dire consequences. The old priest Zacharias was struck dumb for a season because of unbelief:

"And, behold, thou shalt be dumb, and not able to speak, until the day that these things shall be performed, *because thou believest not my words*, which shall be fulfilled in their season." Luke 1:20.

It can even abort God's promises for your life, including that of marriage as we can see from the following scripture below. Here, we are faced with Jesus' inability to do what He had planned in Capernaum, where He grew up, because of their unbelief:

"And he did not many mighty works there because of their unbelief." Matthew 13:58.

If you want to see the blessings that God has promised you come to pass then you should not doubt what He has told you because the word of God says that a double minded person cannot receive anything from God.

"But let him ask in faith, nothing wavering. For he that wavereth is like a wave of the sea driven with the wind and tossed. For let not that man think that he shall receive any thing of the Lord. A double minded man is unstable in all his ways." James 1:6-8.

Another reason you should not doubt the word of God is that doing so implies that God is a liar and not to be trusted. We know that God is trustworthy and cannot lie. **Number 23:19.** To get the promised blessings you should believe what God has told you that He will do for you:

"And blessed is she that believed: for there shall be a performance of those things which were told her from the Lord." Luke 1:45.

Faith without works is dead so your actions should demonstrate your faith in God's word. **James 2:26.** If you truly believe that God is going to give you your own husband then start getting ready for the wedding now. As a work of faith buy that wedding gown, that tuxedo, and other things that you will need for your wedding and marital home. Pray over them regularly until the Lord remembers you and brings His promises to pass in your life. And He shall surely bring them to pass in Jesus name.

This season, the God that located Rebekah and brought her to Isaac will locate your spouse and bring him or her to you in Jesus name. The Lord, who remembered Ruth and gave her Boaz will remember you today and give you your very own custom made spouse in Jesus name. Just remember that God, the Great Provider, has already made provision for "your very own" spouse. Now sit back and be encouraged by this little poem.

MY OWN

Lord you know my own
Lord you chose my own
Lord you have my own
Lord you prepared my own
Lord show me my own
My own, Lord! My own!

Don't have to struggle
Don't have to force
Don't have to fight
Don't have to fret
Lord show me my own
My own, Lord! My own!

My own that accepts me
My own that loves me
My own that appreciates me
My own that desires me
Lord show me my own
My own, Lord! My own!

My own that knows me
My own that knows my worth
My own that knows my heart
My own that knows my needs
Lord give me my own
My own, Lord! My very own!

If you already know who your spouse is but the person is refusing to acknowledge what God is doing then pray the following prayers.

PRAYERS FOR AN UNCOOPERATIVE PARTNER

1. Holy Spirit, You are my helper. Thank you for locating my God-chosen spouse for me in the name of Jesus.
2. Thank you Lord for bringing my God ordained spouse to me. Now, please present me to my God ordained spouse.
3. You my God ordained spouse, see me as your own, and claim me as your own, in the name of Jesus.
4. Every power that has covered the brain of my God ordained partner so that he or she is not thinking right, release it and die.
5. O Lord, open the eyes and ears of my divine partner that he or she may see and hear you clearly concerning this issue.
6. O Lord, glue my divine partner to me in such a way that no power, spirit, or personality can separate us, in the name of Jesus.
7. You my God ordained partner, you will be unable to eat, you will be unable to sleep, and you will not have peace until you do what God has assigned for you to do in my life.

15. FAILURE AT THE EDGE OF SUCCESS

This terrible spirit is also known as the "Spirit of almost there" and the "Spirit of Pisgah." It gets its name from the fact that it was at Pisgah, right at the edge of the Promised Land of Canaan that the Lord showed His servant Moses, the goodness of the Promised Land and then told him that he would neither enter it nor partake of its goodness. **Deuteronomy 34:1-4.** It is a very wicked spirit that allows you to see the good things that God has for your life and marriage but prevents you from entering in and taking possession of them

There are certain factors that energize this spirit. They include evil inheritance; evil verdicts; enchantment; evil covenants; and curses.

This devastating spirit is also known as the "Near success syndrome," because you come very close to your breakthrough but fail to realize it. For example, the Lord may tell you that He is bringing you your life partner. The partner actually shows up but soon after, so does the demon of "Failure at the edge of success." Once this terrible spirit shows up, your great expectations are dashed as the once promising relationship soon fizzles out and dies.

Many of us have languished at this place for years. Today this evil yoke is broken by the reason of the anointing and the siege is over. I prophesy over your life that you are crossing over into your marital Canaan and taking hold of all your marital possession, in the name of Jesus. No power can stop you now. Receive your husband, receive your marital bed, and receive your children, in the miracle working name of Jesus.

PRAYERS FOR FAILURE AT THE EDGE OF BREAKTHROUGHS

1. Every battle raging at the edge of my marital breakthrough, die by fire.
2. Every evil hand stretched forth to abort God's goodness in my life marriage, wither and catch fire in Jesus name.
3. Every serpent and scorpion operating at the edge of my marital breakthroughs, die in the name of Jesus.
4. Every witchcraft power frustrating me at the edge of my marital breakthrough, die now in the name of Jesus.
5. I bind the spirit of almost there troubling my life and marriage and cast it out of my life, in the name of Jesus.
6. Every power behind my seeing good things but not possessing them, you time is up, die now in the name of Jesus.
7. Every wicked power pushing my head down every time that I try to lift it up die the name of Jesus.
8. Any power plucking out good things from my hands, die.
9. Every wicked power making good things to slip out of my hands in the area of marriage, die, in the name of Jesus.
10. Power to acquire good things and keep them, fall upon my life.
11. My Father, let it be known that you are God in my marital 0life, in the name of Jesus.
12. Holy Spirit, connect me to my marital miracle in the name of Jesus.
13. My divine partner, wherever you are appear now in the name of Jesus.
14. Every evil pronouncement, curse, and covenant of "You shall come close to good things, see them, but not partake off them," over my life and marriage, be cancelled by the blood of Jesus.

16. PROCRASTINATION

This is doing tomorrow what you can do today. It has shut the doors of opportunity on the faces of many. When God says "now" and you say "tomorrow" then you are already out of His will and timing. This is because for everything under the sun, there is a time and season. **Ecclesiastes 3:1.** Therefore you should be in tune with divine timing. This entails knowing God's appointed times and seasons for your marriage. God has an appointed time for you to get married. If you miss or squander the opportunity that God gives to you to get married at the appointed time, it may become more difficult if not impossible to get another opportunity.

However, because you are reading this book, which is vomited for those who genuinely want to do it the God way this time around, the God of mercy and many chances will revisit you today and change your marital story to the very best in the name of Jesus.

PRAYER AGAINST THE SPIRIT OF PROCRASTINATION

1. I will not miss God's timing for my marriage, in the mighty name of Jesus.
2. Every satanic bus-stop holding my God ordained partner captive, release him/her and catch fire, in the name of Jesus.
3. Every satanic bus-stop holding me captive, release me, catch fire, and be burnt to ashes, in the name of Jesus.
4. Lord Jesus, arise in your mercy and help me to recover all my wasted years in every area of my life including marriage.
5. Lord Jesus, help me to recover all lost opportunities in the area of marriage.
6. Blood of Jesus, redeem my marital destiny.
7. I refuse to be wasted in the valley of decision, I will get to my Promise Land in the name of Jesus.
8. Everything in me working against the fulfillment of my marital destiny, come out and die now.
9. Every power programming slow progress and sluggishness into my marital destiny, die now.

10. Every power yoking me to satanic delay in marriage, die now.

11. Every yoke of satanic delay targeted at my marriage, break.

12. I pull down every stronghold of satanic delay affecting my getting married with the hands of fire.

13. Every evil programmed into my life and marriage using snails, turtles, millipedes, and okra, be deprogrammed by fire.

14. Every evil calendar and clock running contrary to God's calendar and timing for my life and marriage, catch fire.

15. I impose God's calendar and clock over all evil calendars and timetable contending for my life and marriage.

16. I refuse to cooperate with demotion in the name of Jesus.

17. By the power in the blood of Jesus, I recover back all that I have lost as a result of procrastination in the name of Jesus.

17. LACK OF PREPARATION

"For which of you, intending to build a tower, sitteth not down first, and counteth the cost, whether he have sufficient to finish it? Lest haply, after he hath laid the foundation, and is not able to finish it, all that behold it begin to mock him, Saying, This man began to build, and was not able to finish." Luke 14:28-29.

We learn from the scripture above that for anything to succeed in life there must be planning and preparation. You have to count the cost of any project that you want to undertake in life. Marriage is one of life's most important endeavors, so you should sit down and count the cost before embarking on it.

There are preparations to be made if you want to get married successfully. You have to be mentally, emotionally, physically, and spiritually prepared. For example, if you desire to marry a well-read spouse you should get some level of education yourself. If you need to lose weight or get some decent clothes to look good and presentable, then do so.

Here I have to caution some of our brothers. They have to deal with the worldly spirit which stereotypes genuine Christian women as unglamorous and boring. That is not true at all. There are many healthy,

154

full of zeal, Christian women out there who are a good challenge to any man that is serious about getting a godly wife. However, it is another story if you are looking for a Delilah or a Jezebel. I pray that the Lord will help you to discover who you really are in Christ Jesus in Jesus' name. Until you do that, this book will not help you much because you are heading for destiny diversion and destruction.

If we look at the story of Esther in the Bible, we see that her preparation for marriage was carefully done so that she would please her husband. She was set apart and specially prepared for twelve months. She was cleansed, purged, purified, and beautified:

"Now when every maid's turn was come to go in to king Ahasuerus, after that she had been twelve months, according to the manner of the women, (for so were the days of their purifications accomplished, to wit, six months with oil of myrrh, and six months with sweet odours, and with other things for the purifying of the women;)" Esther 2:12.

How prepared are you today to receive your spouse, the gift that God in His mercy and love has specially packaged for you?

Physically, are you prepared? If God asks you to get married today and it is then that you as a woman start learning how to cook then you are not serious about marriage. It is a well-known secret that the way to a man's heart is through his belly. Can you keep a house? A man once told me that he took a second wife because his wife was a terrible housekeeper regardless of the huge money given to her for housekeeping.

The Bible says a prudent wife is a gift from God. **Proverbs 19:14.** Prudence translates to being God fearing, humble, hardworking, submissive, and knowing how to make your home a haven that the man craves to come back to. You should also keep yourself fit because most men do not want a fat wife. Moreover, it is bad for your health particularly if you plan to have children. Have you lost that weight? May the Lord grant us the grace to do these things, in the name of Jesus! Amen. It is when we do that that our husbands will truly consider us as gifts from God. Anything to the contrary will be more of a burden. Say:

I refuse to be a burden to my spouse in Jesus name.

Financially, are you ready? Sister, if the Lord has told you that your wedding is this summer, why not buy the wedding gown now? Do not let doubt and unbelief rob you of that wedding that you have always dreamt off. Put your plans down on paper and get moving. Get off that couch and go shopping for that wedding dress today because I assure you that by the time that you have finished using this book your story will surely change in Jesus name. Amen!!!!!

You, that brother looking for a wife, are you employed? How do you plan to take care of a wife and children, when they arrive? Will you be running to your parents, siblings, and friends for help every time? If it is when it is time for marriage that you the brother starts saving money and doing other things that you should have done way ahead of time then you are not prepared for marriage.

Spiritually, how prepared are you? How deep are your encounters with God? How deep is your knowledge of the word of God? Do you have a vibrant prayer altar? If you have not built an altar for yourself, how then will you build one for your family? Have you acquired the fire that you will need to fight and win battles in your marriage?

If you are unprepared in any of these basic areas then you are setting yourself up for marital stress, distress, and failure. That will not be our portion this time around in Jesus name. Amen. We will do it right this time. The Almighty God will give us the wisdom and enable us to do it right this time, in Jesus name.

PRAYERS TO PREPARE YOU FOR MARRIAGE

1. O God arise and prepare me for marriage.
2. Holy Spirit you know me more than I know myself, arise and prepare me for marriage.
3. O Lord, as I prepare for marriage disturb the waters of my God ordained spouse. Withdraw his peace, his joy, and his appetite until he comes to claim me as his own.
4. Father let your will be done on earth in my marital life, as it is in heaven.

O GOD ARISE AND BEAUTIFY MY LIFE
(Prayers for God to prepare you for your partner)

1. Power of deliverance, fall upon my life now, in the name of Jesus. (Lay your right hand on your head as you pray this prayer).

2. Holy Spirit, arise take the soap of heaven and the sponge of heaven and give me a divine bath.

3. Holy Spirit, arise and prepare me for the satisfaction of my divine partner after the order of Esther, the wife of Ahasuerus.

4. O Lord, let your glory overshadow and beautify my life in such a way that my God ordain partner will find me irresistible.

5. Holy Spirit, be my hair dresser, dress my hair, and make it beautiful again.

6. Every label and stamp of ugliness put upon my life, catch fire now.

7. Every evil logo that the enemy has put upon my life to make me look old expire by fire. I tear you down.

8. Every serpent that is swallowing my beauty, vomit it and die.

9. Every strange material planted into my body catch fire.

10. O Lord, my Father, by your mercy, bring me out of the room of the forgotten, abandoned, and forsaken, where the enemy has locked me up.

11. God of fire, beautify my life by your fire

12. Let the fragrance of our Lord Jesus Christ, the Rose of Sharon, refresh and beautify my life.

13. Let the resurrection power of our Lord Jesus Christ, renew and beautify my life.

14. I prophesy over my life that the day of my marital fulfillment and glory is now here in the name of Jesus.

15. Holy Spirit, please dress me up to fulfill my marital destiny.

16. Let the beauty of the Lord settle upon my life, in Jesus name.

17. Holy Spirit restore me and make me beautiful for my spouse.

18. ANTI-GLORY POWERS (Isaiah 60:1-2)

Please pray the following prayers:

1. My hidden glory, appear now and shine for the world to see.
2. My glory is not for sale, if my glory has been sold off, let the blood of Jesus repossess it for me now.
3. You my buried marital glory, hear the word of the Lord, wherever you have been buried (mention them one by one e.g. in the waters, forest, heavenlies, rock, tree, ground), be exhumed and locate me now, in the name of Jesus.
4. You my stolen marital glory, I recover you back by fire and by force.
5. All anti-glory forces assigned against my marriage lose your hold upon my life, in Jesus' name.

Anti-glory powers are star killers, who do not want people to shine in life, including the area of marriage. They waste people's potentials and virtues and rob them of their marital glory. Anti-glory powers include diviners, satanic agents, stubborn spirit spouses, enchanters, and witchcraft powers. They exchange, bury, shave off, or sell off people's marital glory. They are the ancestral strongmen that confiscate person's glory and store it in their warehouses. They are the marine powers that specialize in trading with, burying, or satanically exchanging people's glory and virtues. They delight in relocating a person from the head to the tail region and from being first to being last. They want you to settle for less than what God's says that you are in every area of life including marriage.

Any dream about your hair is talking about your glory and your covering and so should be taken seriously. Dreams involving hair not looking good or needing to be fixed; dirty or unkempt hair; and someone cutting off your hair should be handled immediately with violent prayers and when possible deliverance. So should dreams of rain falling on you and messing up your hair. You should invite the Holy Spirit to be your divine hair dresser and dress you up to fulfill your marital destiny. Ask Him to restore you and make you beautiful for your spouse. Any dream about head gears, hats, and scarves being stolen, taken, or blown away should be fought aggressively with the right prayers as well.

All dreams of nakedness, particularly before one's God ordained spouse, should be taken seriously. So should dreams of being around feces or urine. They are meant to introduce pollution, rejection, shame, reproach, disgrace, and disappointment into your life and marital destiny. They are anti-glory dreams that indicate that your glory has been exposed to shame, poverty, and rejection.

Now, we have to pray to recover our lost, stolen, exchanged, buried, battered, and vandalized glory. Are you ready? Then pray the following prayers as if your life and marriage depends on it.

PRAYERS FOR MAKING MARITAL GLORY TO SHINE

1. Anti-shining powers of my father's house, assigned against my marriage, die now, in the mighty name of Jesus.
2. Anti-shining powers of my mother's house, assigned against my marriage, die, in Jesus name.
3. Anti-shining powers in my environment, assigned against my marriage, die by fire, in Jesus name.
4. Anti-shining powers from my place of birth or origin assigned against my marriage, die by fire.
5. Every power with evil awareness of my marital destiny, die, in the name of Jesus.
6. Every evil wall surrounding my marital glory, be demolished by the dynamite thunder of God.
7. You my marital glory reject satanic manipulation, evil exchange, and transfer, in the mighty name of Jesus.
8. Every Delilah assigned to shave off my Samson, die.
9. Any satanic burial done against my marital glory, be reversed now.
10. All my buried marital glory, be exhumed now in Jesus' name.
11. Every power gathered against my glory, wherever you are, whoever you are, perish by fire.

12. Evil clouds of darkness gathering over my marital destiny, clear away.

13. Light of God, disperse any darkness covering my marital glory.

14. Power to shine in my marital life, fall upon me now.

15. Household witchcraft powers holding unto my glory, release it and die.

16. My glory what are you doing in the dustbin of life, rise up and shine.

17. Wicked powers blocking me from shining, I bury you now, in the name of Jesus.

18. Witchcraft barbers that have shaved off my marital glory, restore it and die.

19. Monitoring gadgets assigned against my marital destiny, catch fire and be roasted to ashes.

20. Every power dragging my glory on the ground, die now.

21. Every power assigned to turn my marital glory to shame, die by fire.

22. Satanic hands manipulating my marital glory, wither in the name of Jesus.

23. My marital glory, awake and explode by fire, in the name of Jesus.

24. All the glory that I carry will not turn to shame in Jesus' name

25. Wicked ancestors seating on my marital glory, be unseated and die, in the name of Jesus.

26. Every evil rain assigned to afflict my marital life, dry up by fire.

27. Every marine onslaught against my glory, die now.

28. God of restoration visit me today and restore my glory.

29. Violent angels from heaven, search through the land of the living and the dead and recover all my lost, transferred, and stolen marital glory.

30. I recall and recover all my marital blessings thrown into the water, the forest, and satanic banks.

19. ANTI-HARVEST POWERS (ISAIAH 65:19-24)

Anti-harvest powers are very wicked powers that allow you to sow and work hard towards fulfilling your marital destiny. They allow you to gather good things towards your marital fulfillment and victory and then just as you are about tie the knots they strike and scatter everything that you have labored to gather. They empty out all the virtues and potentials that you have worked hard for. Close your eyes and pray this prayer:

Every power, spirit, or personality that has stolen my marital harvest, return it, and die, in the name of Jesus.

These powers wait patiently while you pray the prayers to know the will of God; to identify your spouse; and to get connected. Everything seems to be going well. They watch as you invest in prayers and fasting; encourage your partner; and sow in time and other resources into his or her life. Then when it is time to get married these powers strike and take over everything that you worked hard for.

They may come as strong men and confiscate the fruit of your labor, locking it up in their strong-room and denying you access to it. Today the power of God will destroy all such strong-rooms and bring to you your blessings stored there.

They also appear as demoting powers that are on assignment to reposition you from the first to the last, from the mountain top to the valley, and from the front to the back. They make you, the favored one, to become the rejected one. They render your hard work profitless because your God ordained spouse marries someone else right before your very eyes. In a moment, the power of the emptier can empty out everything that you have worked for in a marital relationship for months and even years. Please make the following confessions:

1. I am the first, I will not become the last, in Jesus name."
2. Every strongman assigned to relocate me from the front to the back, fall down and die now.
3. Every ancient old woman troubling my life and marital destiny, fall down and die, in the name of Jesus.

4. Power to locate my divine marital placement, fall on me now.

5. O God, arise and reposition me for marital success.

Anti-harvest powers can come as devourers and devour everything that you have worked hard for. The power of the spoiler spoils your harvest by polluting the relationship. He also makes both of you to start seeing each other as the enemy while the real the enemy, the devil, is busy destroying the colorful marriage that God had ordained for you.

Anti-harvest powers program evil things into once blossoming relationships. They come as wasters that waste time, efforts, and destinies. They appear as spiritual gunmen in your dreams shooting at you. They come as satanic policemen in the dream to handcuff you and arrest your marital progress; and as satanic gatemen mounting evil gates to divert your marital destiny. They program cobwebs into your life to divert your partner and make the relationship go stale overnight. They appear as ancestral rats and devour your possessions. They come also as demonic birds and eat up your harvest and your partner's love for you.

Be encouraged because even now, it is not too late. You must refuse to give an inch to these wicked powers. You have to fight back and take control of that marital relationship again. Whatever it takes, fasting, prayers, or deliverance you should ensure that power changes hands again to the hands of the Holy Spirit in your marital destiny. Before we pray, let us make these eight additional confessions:

1. I will not sow and another reap, in the mighty name of Jesus.

2. I will not build and another inhabit, in the name of Jesus.

3. In my marriage, I will not bring forth for trouble, in Jesus name.

4. I will not labor in vain, and my harvest will not be stolen.

5. I will eat the fruits of the vineyard that I have planted.

6. Another person will not occupy my marital seat, Jesus name.

7. All my investment in my marital destiny will not be in vain.

8. Another will not drink the water assigned to me and my marriage.

PRAYERS TO CRUSH ANTI-HARVEST POWERS

1. My marital harvest manifest by fire
2. I shall not labor in vain in my marital life in the name of Jesus.
3. Within 24 hours my marital promotion appear by fire in the name of Jesus.
4. Every power seating on my harvest, be unseated by fire and die, in the name of Jesus.
5. Any power assigned to withhold my marital harvest and celebration this year, you are a failure, die.
6. Anti-harvest powers assigned against my marital breakthrough, your time is up die, now.
7. Spirit of profitless hard work, my life is not your candidate, therefore die by fire, in the name of Jesus.
8. Every covenant of profitless hard work in my foundation, break and die, in the name of Jesus.
9. O God, after the order of Ruth, arise and use me to rewrite my family history.
10. Wasters, devourers, emptiers, and spoilers assigned against my marriage, your time is up, die by fire.
11. Any power that has stolen, exchanged, or destroyed my marital harvest, release my harvest and die.
12. Every door that has been opened to devourers in my marital life and destiny, be closed by the blood of Jesus.
13. Every power assigned to embarrass and put me to shame in the area of marriage, die.
14. Powers militating against my God ordained marital fulfillment and uplifting, die by fire.
15. Everything in me cooperating with anti-harvest powers, come out and die, in the name of Jesus.
16. O Lord, contend with every power contesting with me for my marital seat, in the name of Jesus.
17. You my stolen or destroyed marital harvest be restored by the blood of Jesus, in the name of Jesus.

20. SPIRITUAL BLINDNESS AND DEAFNESS (ISAIAH 6:9-10)

"Where there is no vision, the people perish." Proverbs 29:18.

"Hear ye indeed, but understand not; and see ye indeed, but perceive not. Make the heart of this people fat, and make their ears heavy, and shut their eyes; lest they see with their eyes, and hear with their ears, and understand with their heart, and convert, and be healed." Isaiah 6:9-10.

A man is a spirit being that has a soul and lives in a body. A man should be able to see in all three realms. Spiritual blindness is the inability to see with your spiritual eyes what is happening in the spirit realm. This affects your ability to take hold of the good things that God has for you in the area of marriage. This is because if you are unable to see the breakthroughs that God has for you while they are still in the spirit realm, it will be very difficult to take delivery of them in the physical realm. This Bible reinforcing this says that as a man thinks in his heart so is he. **Proverbs 23:7.** What do you see in your mind's eyes today concerning your marriage? Do you see a bright marital destiny or do you see loneliness, sorrow, disappointment, and rejection?

Spiritual deafness, likewise, also hinders a person from receiving from the Lord. It is when you are unable to hear in the spirit realm. God is a spirit and talks to our spirit man. Your spiritual ears should be ready to receive instructions Him daily that will move your marital life forward. **(Isaiah 50:40).**

When a person can neither see nor hear, the Bible describes such a person as being asleep or slumbering. **Romans 11:8.** This is a very dangerous because while you are busy sleeping, the enemy can catch up with you and steal, kill and destroy precious things in your marital life. God can restore lost things to us but sometimes some things are lost forever. For example, Samson lost his hair and his eyes while slumbering. He got his hair back but never recovered his eyes until he died. **Judges 16:21.**

Today, God's grace and mercy are available to deliver you from the spirit of deafness and blindness. Receive new eyes to see into your future and new ears to receive divine instructions that will move your marital life forward in Jesus name

PRAYERS TO REMOVE SPIRITUAL BLINDNESS AND DEAFNESS

1. Every spiritual cataract in my eyes preventing me from seeing clearly what God has for me in marriage, clear away by fire.
2. Every spiritual wax in my ears blocking me from hearing God concerning my life and marriage, melt away.
3. Every embargo put on my getting married, break and die.
4. Every power tampering with my marital star, be disgraced.
5. Every power confusing my God ordained spouse and preventing him from recognizing me as his own, scatter.
6. Let the power to recognize my divine partner fall upon me.
7. Let the power to recognize me as his/her own fall upon my divine partner.
7. Any darkness planned for me by the enemy, go back to your sender.
8. I fire back every arrow of spiritual blindness, in Jesus name.
9. I fire back every arrow of spiritual deafness, in the name of Jesus.
10. Every evil bird assigned to blind me, fall down and die.
11. Spirit of error and mistake, my life is not your candidate, clear away by fire.
12. Every power of bewitchment troubling the life of my partner die.
13. Every power of bewitchment troubling my life, die.
14. You, my marital life, refuse to be bewitched.
15. You my God ordained partner, refuse to be deceived.
16. I refuse to be deceived in the area of marriage.
17. O Lord, open my eyes that I may see, in the name of Jesus.
18. O Lord, open my ears that I may hear, in the name of Jesus.

21. NEGATIVE CONFESSIONS

"Say unto them, as I live, saith the Lord, as ye have spoken in mine ears, so will I do to you." **Numbers 14:28.**

"For verily I say unto you, That whosoever shall say unto this mountain, Be thou removed, and be thou cast into the sea; and shall not doubt in his heart, but shall believe that those things which he saith shall come to pass; he shall have whatsoever he saith." **Mark 11:23.**

God spoke the whole of the universe into being by the power of His word. **Hebrews 1:3.** A closed mouth is a closed destiny. So today, you should open your mouth confess what the word of God says about your marital situation, not the facts or what you are feeling at the particular time. Your confessions should agree with the pictures that God is showing you in your mind concerning your marital life. If you know who your God ordained spouse is and he is acting contrary to what God has told or shown you, you should not let his behavior change your confessions unless the Lord tells you otherwise. God expects His children to walk by faith and not by sight. **2 Corinthians 5:7.** The Bible says that we are justified or condemned by our words.

"For by thy words thou shalt be justified, and by thy words thou shalt be condemned." **Matthew 12:37.**

Therefore, under no circumstance should you speak negative things about your situation or yourself. These include statements such as, "Who would want a 46 year old woman as a wife?"; "Who would marry a woman like me?" "No woman would want a loser like me." The Bible says also, that out of the abundance of the heart the mouth speaks. **Matthew 12:34.** That being the case, you should fill yourself with the word of God so that wholesome words will flow out of your heart and then come out of your mouth always as you speak.

22. BAD ATTITUDE AND BAD CHARACTER

A bad attitude and a bad character turn off people, including prospective spouses. It also gives you a bad report and makes you a bad witness for Christ.

A bad attitude includes complaining, murmuring, bitterness, unforgiveness, anger, irritability, lack of contentment, laziness, gloom, comparing yourself with others, unappreciative and unthankful attitude, bad manners, unhealthy competition, lack of home training, and lack of basic social etiquette.

A bad character includes lack of integrity, lying, stealing, drug addiction, loose behavior with the opposite sex, and drinking.

If you have issues like the ones mentioned above, you should prayerfully deal with them and seek counseling and deliverance when needed. You should also mend your ways so that you do not sink your marital ship. Pray like this:

1. **If I am my own problem, Holy Spirit, help me to do it right this time, in the name of Jesus.**
2. **Every negative pattern, characteristic, behavior, habits, traits, and leanings working against my marital breakthroughs, be arrested by the blood of Jesus.**
3. **Internal stumbling blocks delaying my marital progress come out and die in the name of Jesus.**

23. IMPATIENCE

There is an appointed time for the fulfillment of every promise of God for our lives. **Ecclesiastes 3:4.** Always remember that the vision that God has given to you for your marriage is for an appointed time. At the fullness of time the marriage will manifest in the physical. This means that you have to be patient and be able to endure in order to receive the fullness of your breakthrough, and not end up with just a portion of it.

"For ye have need of patience that after ye have done the will of God, ye might receive the promise." Hebrew 10:36.

**"And so, after he had patiently endured, he obtained the promise."
Hebrews 6:15.**

You should not let impatience slaughter your marital destiny. The
Bible writes for our encouragement that:

**"Better is the end of a thing than the beginning thereof: and the
patient in spirit is better than the proud in spirit." Ecclesiastes 7:8.**

Even when it appears as if the relationship is over because that
marine witchcraft agent has entrenched herself in your partner's life, you
should still wait patiently on the Lord. You should trust Him that He will
fulfill His promises in your life. You should rest on Him completely and
put your full confidence in Him alone:

**"Rest in the LORD, and wait patiently for him: fret not thyself
because of him who prospereth in his way, because of the man who
bringeth wicked devices to pass." Psalm 37:7.**

**"I waited patiently for the LORD; and he inclined unto me, and
heard my cry." Psalm 40:1.**

Let us take the following prayer together:

**Every power behind marital problems in my life, I bury you now, in
the name of Jesus. (Repeat over and over "I bury you now.")**

24. STINGINESS

"There is that scattereth, and yet increaseth; and there is that withholdeth more than is meet, but it tendeth to poverty." **Proverbs 11:24.**

Stinginess is the inability to give. There is a law of sowing and reaping; of seed time and harvest time. **Genesis 8:22.** You should sow into your marital destiny so you can reap a bumper harvest in return. If you eat your seed then there can be no harvest in due season.

You can sow in various ways such as in vows and special offerings. The less is always blessed by the greater. **Hebrew 7:7.** So, you can sow into the work of God or into the life of God's anointed servants. Every month you can bless the men and women of God around you. Whenever possible have them pray for your marriage. You should also be a blessing to others around you particularly the less privileged and the needy. **Isaiah 58:7.** You should not be a closed pipe that nothing flows through because it leads to stagnancy and staleness in all areas of life including marriage. Sow a seed into your marital destiny today and expect a bountiful harvest.

A good way to provoke God to move speedily on your behalf is to make a vow. A vow is promise that you make to God that when He does a specific thing that you have asked Him to do, that you in return will do a specified thing in return. It could be that you will make an offering of $500 if He gets you married. It could be to clean the church for a year. It is an agreement between you and God. Please do not make any vow that you cannot keep as failure to redeem your vow will bring you under a curse. **Ecclesiastes 5:4-5.** You should only make a vow if you are sure that you will be able to redeem it. You can redeem it before or after God does His part of the bargain by getting you married.

25. SATANIC DIVERSION (ISAIAH 54:16-17)

Satanic diversion is any step that you take that takes you away from the purpose and destiny that God' has for your life. It is when evil powers make you go in the opposite direction from where God wants you to go at any particular time and in any given situation.

In the area of marriage, it is when the enemy and his cohorts want to take you on a marital journey that God has not ordained for you. God can ordain for you to marry Mr. B, but satanic powers can divert you to marry Mr. A, just to keep you from God's agenda for your life and to abort your destiny and short change you. The sad thing is that while you are busy going off tangent, your peers catch up with you, pass you, and leave you behind. It makes a journey of two weeks to take forty years of going around in circles; marking time in one spot; and achieving nothing.

If you are seeing satanic gatekeepers and cobwebs in your dreams or even in the physical as well, then you need to pray seriously against satanic diversion, blockages, and the spirit of error and mistake. If you are being driven by an unknown person to an unknown destination, then you are a student in the school of satanic diversion. You have to pray yourself out of it with diligence. I pray that this time around you will refuse to obey any evil command in Jesus name.

PRAYERS AGAINST SATANIC DIVERSION

Song: 1. I will reach my goal Alleluia. 2. I will get to my Promise Land.

1. Power to locate my divine marital location in life, fall upon me now, in the name of Jesus.
2. Every power programming confusion into my marital life, die now.
3. Evil magnets, attracting the wrong people to me melt away by fire.
4. Evil magnets, be replaced by good magnets in my marital life.
5. I refuse to be diverted from my marital destiny.

170

6. Every power, personality, or spirit assigned to divert my marital destiny, die.

7. Every arrow of error and mistake fired into my marital destiny, my life is not your candidate, backfire.

8. Every vagabond anointing dry up by fire and die.

9. Every arrow of confusion, jump out and backfire.

10. Every power making me to move around in circles in my marital destiny, die now.

11. Powers sowing confusion into my marital destiny, your time is up, fall down and die, now.

12. Any power pushing me to marry whom God has not ordained for me to marry, lose your hold and die, in the name of Jesus.

13. Powers blocking me from reaching my marital goal, die.

14. Every power assigned to take me back to square one, you are a liar, die.

15. I .... (Put your name here) turn back from every journey into marital darkness.

16. Every evil gang up and decision taken against my marriage scatter by fire.

17. I refuse to obey any satanic instructions contrary to my God ordained marriage.

18. Every witchcraft vehicle and driver assigned to divert my martial destiny, I separate my life from you and I set you on fire.

19. Every satanic cobweb and spider assigned to arrest or to divert my marital destiny, catch fire and be roasted to ashes.

20. No divination, enchantment, or incantations will work against my life and marriage, in the name of Jesus.

21. All satanic traffic wardens diverting good things away from me, be paralyzed by fire, in the name of Jesus.

26. **EVIL GATES (JOSHUA 6:1-20, PSALM 24:7, PSALM 107:16, GENESIS 28:11-17, MATTHEW 16:18-19)**

"I will go before thee, and make the crooked places straight: I will break in pieces the gates of brass, and cut in sunder the bars of iron" Isaiah 45:2.

Gates are very significant in a person's life. They are entering points into such a life either for goodness or evil. They are important because promotion takes place first in the spiritual realm before it manifests in the physical. In the spiritual realm, to move from one position to another; one level to another; or from one location to another; you have to pass through a gate. Terrible demonic powers guard these gates to hinder God's children from going in to take possession of their blessings. Satanic gatemen also man these gates to keep people locked up in prison and bad situations. This is to prevent them from coming out to enjoy God's goodness for their lives including marriage.

Evil spiritual gates include witchcraft, ancestral, familiar spirit, and marine gates. There are gates in all three spiritual realms which are the heavens, the earth, and underneath the earth. In these realms, decisions are made about people's marital destinies and wicked powers seriously contend against people's marriages.

PRAYERS TO DEMOLISH EVIL GATES

1. Every evil gate that has locked up my God ordained spouse, open by fire, open by force in Jesus name.
2. Every evil gate preventing me from taking possession of my marital breakthroughs, open by thunder, in the name of Jesus.
3. Evil gates, bars, and walls separating me from my God ordained spouse, open by fire, in the name of Jesus.
4. Every evil gate and gatekeeper keeping me away from my God ordained spouse, fall down and die.

5. You the gate of marital breakthrough closed against my life, open by fire, in the name of Jesus.

6. Blood of Jesus overturn all evil decisions and decrees taken against my life and marriage at any evil gate.

7. Every wicked elder deliberating against my life and marriage at any gate, receive the judgment of God.

8. Every evil gathering holding at any wicked gate against my life and marriage, scatter unto desolation, in the name of Jesus.

9. I declare by the blood of Jesus that the gates of hell shall not prevail against my life and marriage in Jesus name.

10. My Father, my Father, my Father where I have no voice, raise up a voice to speak for me at the gate.

11. Evil sacrifices, rituals, and other wicked operations carried out against my marital destiny at satanic gates backfire in the name of Jesus.

12. All ancestral and tribal gates and doors militating against my marital breakthrough, be uprooted and roasted to ashes.

13. By the power in the blood of Jesus, I decree that no one shall say to me, "sorry, try again next time" in the area of marriage.

14. Every gate of marital breakthrough closed against me open by fire.

15. Every evil gate in the heavens blocking my marital breakthrough, be dismantled by thunder.

16. Every evil gate on earth blocking my marital progress, be melted away by fire.

17. Every evil gate underneath the earth blocking my marital breakthroughs and testimonies break and die.

18. Every gate in the waters blocking my marriage, break now.

19. Every battle raging at evil gates against my marriage scatter, by fire, in the name of Jesus.

20. Blood of Jesus repair every damage done to my marital destiny at evil gates.

27. INCOMPLETE DELIVERANCE

"But upon mount Zion shall be deliverance, and there shall be holiness; and the house of Jacob shall possess their possessions." Obadiah 1:17.

How complete is your deliverance? Sister, are you still having sex in the dream every night? And now you want to marry a brother that is doing the same? You both need to deal with the situation first through deliverance before going into marriage. Otherwise, marrying him will compound both of your problems. This is because all unresolved deliverance issues that you bring into the marriage will be transferred to your spouse and vice versa. This means that all his demons and problems will become yours and yours his, thereby magnifying the problems. It is very important therefore to ensure that your deliverance is complete before venturing into marriage.

Incomplete deliverance hinders the good things that God wants to do in various areas in a person's life as it keeps serious problems in place. A person whose deliverance is not complete will experience afflictions and oppressions repeating themselves whereas the Bible says that affliction should not arise again a second time. **Nahum 1:9**. The result is that the person will keep rising and fall and going round in circles.

Your deliverance is not complete if the problems for which you previously went for deliverance ministration are still in place. These include problems such as rejection, spirit spouse, hatred, disappointment, stagnancy, and bad-luck. The Bible says that whom the Son sets free, is free indeed. **John 8:36.** Total and absolute deliverance is available through Christ Jesus. Therefore, you should go back for a comprehensive deliverance and be completely set free.

Your dreams to a large extent also indicate whether your deliverance is complete or not. Are your dreams bringing you divine revelations that will move your life forward or is it the opposite? Are all that you see in your dreams dead people; naked men and women; snakes pursuing you; dogs biting you; sex in the dream; eating in the dream; talking to old school mates; wearing old high school uniforms; cobwebs trailing you;

174

and precious things being stolen from you? Then obviously your deliverance is not complete. You should go for deliverance today. **(Please call the telephone number at the back of the book for referrals).**

One very important area to deal with thoroughly through deliverance before venturing into marriage is your foundation. Foundational deliverance is particularly important because your marriage can only be as strong as your foundation. A faulty foundation cannot carry a good marriage, just like weak pillars cannot carry a building. Therefore, you have to ensure through deliverance that your foundation is strong enough to sustain a healthy marriage. So before treading into matrimony you should clean up your foundation and ensure that it is resting solidly on Christ Jesus the solid Rock and His principles as presented in the Bible. He is the only foundation on which you can build that never fails.

Cleaning up your foundation before going into a marital relationship will help to resolve common problems often encountered before marriage. These include inability to get married, satanic delay, constant rejection and disappointment, error and mistake, and attraction to wrong partners. It will also put in place a new and sound foundation built on Christ Jesus that can carry a good marriage and minimize common problems often encountered in marriage such as barrenness, misunderstandings, financial problems, harassment from in-laws, loneliness, divorce, and untimely death.

Deliverance will help you to live a holy life. It will also bring restoration which will provoke breakthroughs in various areas of your life including marriage. **Obadiah 1:17.**

Deliverance, above all, will put in your hands divine secrets that will move your life and marital destiny forward. As you plug into a good deliverance program, you will receive divine attention and solution to your marital challenges in Jesus name.

PRAYERS TO ARREST ANTI-DELIVERANCE POWERS

Song: Fire of God fall upon me.

1. Every power behind rising and falling in my life, fall down and die in Jesus name.
2. Every power keeping problems in place in life, release me and die, in the name of Jesus.
3. Evil hands and legs working about for my sake, I cut you off now, in the name of Jesus.
4. Every evil altar and priest working against my total and absolute deliverance, catch fire and be roasted to ashes in the name of Jesus.
5. Everything in my foundation working against my deliverance, come out and die, in the name of Jesus.
6. Every circle of problems in my life, die, in Jesus name.
7. I shall not give up, my problems shall give up.
8. You powers working against my total and absolute deliverance and testimonies, fall down and die, in the name of Jesus.
9. O lord save me and I shall be saved, heal me and I shall be healed, and deliver me by your outstretched hand.
10. Every yoke of rising and falling, break by the power of God.
11. By the power in the blood of Jesus, I declare and I decree that total and permanent deliverance is mine in the name of Jesus.
12. By the power in the blood of Jesus I declare that my deliverance shall be permanent.

28. SATANIC TRIGGERS

Satanic triggers are physical and spiritual occurrences, which spark off problems in a person's life. They can start off problems in a promising marital relationship which hitherto enjoyed peace, love, and harmony. For example, some people see snakes, lizards, or crocodiles in their dreams and problems start in various areas of their lives including marriage. Some have even run mad after seeing these satanic animals. Others have sex in the dream and good things in their lives, including the area of marriage, start dying for no apparent reason. Expected breakthroughs and blessings that had seemed so sure are aborted and no longer materialize after these strange experiences.

There are also physical things that trigger both spiritual and physical problems. For example, some people wear wigs and human hair attachments and they trigger insanity. In others, wearing them triggers vicious sexual attacks in the dream. The sexual encounter in the dream in turn triggers the abortion of good things in the physical including promising marital relationships, jobs, and contracts. It is truly a vicious circle that must be broken.

However, there is hope for you today, because the Bible says that upon Mount Zion there shall be deliverance, and there shall be holiness, after which you shall indeed possess your possessions including marriage in Jesus name. **Obadiah 1:17**. Please pray the following prayers with aggression:

1. Holy Ghost judgment, descend on every evil trigger planted into my life.
2. Triggers of darkness troubling my life and marriage, your time is up, catch fire.
3. Dream triggers, scatter by fire, in the name of Jesus.

29. DREAM ATTACKS

"But while men slept, his enemy came and sowed tares among the wheat, and went his way." Matthew 13:25.

Once again, the rule is that the spirit realm controls the physical realm. Therefore, if things go wrong in the spirit realm and they are not corrected quickly through prayers and deliverance, then problems will start manifesting in the physical. The enemy normally uses terrible attacks in the dream as a major weapon to bring trouble into the lives of God's children. The area of marriage is not different. For some sisters, whenever men show interest in marrying them, they start having terrible dreams attacks. These attacks include sex with known and unknown partners; being pressed down or vandalized in the dream; and head gears, shoes, or other precious things stolen. Some brothers are beaten up in their dreams by jealous spirit spouses. All these are manifestations of warfare at the edge of marital breakthrough. It is a battle with the spirit of Pisgah, which is also known as the spirit of "Almost there" or "Near success syndrome." The result can be very devastating as a once robust marital relationship can suddenly fizzle out and die.

If you are having serious dream attacks then you should pray dream conditioning prayers. **(Call the number at the back of this book to inquire about these**) If these bring no relief, you should go for deliverance.

30. SATANIC DEFILEMENT (ZECHARIAH 3:1-5)

"For thou wilt not leave my soul in hell; neither wilt thou suffer thine Holy One to see corruption." Psalm 16:9-11

Another weapon that the enemy uses to disrupt a person's marital destiny is spiritual pollution or defilement. Defilement is one of the tares that the enemy sows among the wheat in the garden of a person's life in order to create problems. **Matthew 13:25.**

Defilement pushes good things, including marriage, far away from a person. This is because God will not have anything to do with a polluted person until such a person is cleaned up. We see this play out in the life of Joshua the high priest in **Zechariah 3:1-5**. God had to send an angel to deal with the pollution by removing Joshua's filthy and polluted garments before He could have anything to do with him. The problem of defilement should be handled with great urgency because it separates a person from God and His goodness, and hinders prayers.

Many singles get to the edge of major marital breakthroughs and then the enemy comes along and defiles them. This resulting pollution triggers the abortion of the breakthroughs which were just around the corner. There are various ways that the enemy can defile a person's life.

One way is through evil associations. If you keep polluted friends, they will pollute you. **2 Corinthians 6:17.** The enemy can also come in through your dreams and visions to defile your body, soul, and spirit. You may start seeing objects that defile a person in your dreams such as feces; male and female sexual organs; or people having sex. You may also be subjected with or without your consent to activities that defile such as eating, drinking, and having sex in the dream. You may be spat, urinated, or excreted on in the dream. Pray like this:

Any power spitting, urinating, and defecating on my destiny, your time is up, fall down and die, in the name of Jesus.

Pollution, whether in the spiritual or in the physical realm, triggers problems in the spiritual as well as in the physical lives of victims just like it did in the life of Joshua the priest that was mentioned above. These problems include sudden hatred, reproach, shame, disappointment, rejection, and failure particularly at the edge of marital breakthroughs. It can make formerly cooperative suitors to suddenly lose interest in the relationship for no reason or to abscond. The result is an unending cycle of disappointment, rejection, abandonment, and frustration.

Some years back, the Lord told a sister that He was bringing her a spouse from Europe. The man showed up and they became very good friends. While they were just friends there was no problem but the moment that he expressed interest in marrying her, the demonic attacks started. She started seeing feces and urine in her dreams. The effect soon started manifesting in the physical as for no apparent reason the brother started withdrawing. Evil counselors dealt the final blow to the relationship. The young man eventually married a younger lady. The sad thing is that he met the younger lady before he ever met the older sister and expressed interest in marrying her. If you truly believe that enough is enough of these kinds of problems, please join me in praying these prayers. Pray them as if your life depends on it.

**1. I smash to pieces every demonic mirror monitoring my marriage.
2. Every pollution to my marital breakthrough, be washed away by the blood of Jesus.
3. Let all contamination and pollution introduced into my life through dreams, be purged by fire and flushed out by the blood of Jesus, in the name of Jesus.**

4. I command every spiritual contamination in my life to receive cleansing and healing in Jesus name.

6. Every power that wants me to die in this condition, die now.

7. Every power assigned to waste my marital destiny, die.

31. BLACK MAGIC AND THE OCCULT

Practicing black magic and occultism is expressly forbidden by God. **Deuteronomy 18:14.** It is tapping into a power source which is not of God and is an illegal way to enter the spirit realm. **John 10:1.** There is only one door through which Christians are allowed to access the spirit realm and that door is our Lord Jesus Christ. **John 10:9.** Increasingly, these days many people including "Christians" are dabbling into the occult and witchcraft. Even in the so called civilized places like America and Europe, many are doing so too. This has become even more so since the advent of the Harry Porter movies which glamourized witchcraft. These people fail to realize the damage that witchcraft and anything connected to it will do not only to their lives but also to the lives of their children including those yet unborn.

Some consult psychics; magicians; palmists; wizards; warlocks; familiar spirit and marine powered priests and pastors; and other occult media to acquire power, wealth, knowledge, or to get their problems solved. Some acquire love portions to bewitch unsuspecting men and women and to manipulate them into marriage. Others donate their blood and the blood of their boyfriends or girlfriends for rituals to manipulate them into marriage or to bring back runaway partners.

All these are open doors and ladders that bring strange and devastating problems into such lives. They abort the glorious destiny that God originally planned for such lives. You cannot mix any other power with Jesus. **1 Corinthians 10:21.** It is either He is able or He is not. You cannot seat on the fence or Jesus will spew you out. **Revelation 3:15-16.** Pray like this:

Every strange power, strange mirror, and strange candle attacking my life and marriage, shatter to pieces, in the name of Jesus.

DO IT RIGHT THIS TIME

PRAYERS AGAINST EVIL TRIGGERS, POLLUTION, AND DEFILEMENT

Songs: 1. Holy Ghost possess me by fire. 2. Holy Ghost fire fall on me.

1. Masquerading powers working against my life and marriage be exposed and disgraced.
2. O God, arise and judge every enemy of my marriage today.
3. You power of defilement, my life is not your candidate, die now.
4. Plantations of defilement in my body, come out with all your roots by fire.
5. I cancel the manifestation of every satanic dream.
6. Every evil animal on an errand to pollute my life, die.
7. Every power attacking me at the edge of my miracles, die now.
8. Every strongman behind repeated problems in my life, die.
9. Blood of Jesus, sanitize every organ in my body from demonic pollution.
10. Anything in my body, that is making the enemy to return, I disconnect you now, in the name of Jesus.
11. Every stranger in my body, come out by fire, in Jesus name.
12. Evil eyes monitoring my life receive the fire of God and go blind.
13. Holy Spirit, send your military angels to fight my battles for me.
14. Holy Ghost judgment, descend on every evil trigger planted in my life.
15. Triggers of darkness, your time is up, catch fire, in the name of Jesus.
16. Any power protecting my enemies, I break your backbone, die, in Jesus name.
17. Every personality, spirit, and power carrying out evil sacrifices and rituals for my sake, reap the evil consequences, in Jesus name.
18. Evil hands carrying sacrifice and doing enchantment for my sake, I cut you off with the sword of God.
19. Every completed work of darkness against me and my marriage, be nullified by the blood of Jesus.

32. EVIL MARITAL YOKES (MARK 5:1-20, Matthew 11:28-30, JERIEMIAH 30:7, ISAIAH 10:27)

"And it shall come to pass in that day, that his burden shall be taken away from off thy shoulder, and his yoke from off thy neck, and the yoke shall be destroyed because of the anointing." Isaiah 10:27.

Say seven hot times: "Today, every stubborn yoke in my marital life shall be broken."

A yoke is an instrument that ties two animals together in order to pull a load. The actions and movement of one animal affects the other animal. A yoke is an instrument that the enemy has used to destroy many colorful marital destinies. Today it shall be destroyed because no weapon fashioned against you shall prosper. **Isaiah 54:17.**

An evil marital yoke is an evil load hanging on a person's marital destiny. It allows the enemy to oppress such a life. It brings circular problems. It is anything limiting your progress. It is a satanic chain binding a person's life and making such a one unavailable for marriage. It separates you from your marital breakthroughs. It weighs you down, keeping you from rising matrimonially. It determines the amount and quality of progress that you make in the area of marriage. It may be a yoke that you will not settle down in life or that you will never marry.

The problem is that you may be laboring under an evil yoke and not even know it. This is because some yokes are hidden and are just waiting until their maturity date to manifest. Evil yokes can come from a person's foundation. They can be inherited from one's ancestors. Yokes can be transferred into a person's life by a stronger power.

There are certain factors that keep stubborn marital yokes in place in a person's life. One is a faulty foundation. Another is sex outside of marriage. Worldliness also keeps them in place. Negative confessions fuel evil yokes. Backsliding and going back to your old vomit will keep them waxing strong. A desert spiritual life energizes them. This is a life style of no discipline with no prayers, no vigils, no fasting, no quiet time, no Bible study and skipping of church services. These all culminates in a person not carrying any fire. Without fire, the devil is able to have a field day in such a life.

Today, there is hope for you. The Bible tells us that the anointing can break every yoke that is harassing your marital destiny. As you pray the following prayers that anointing will step in and break all the yokes troubling your marital destiny and set you free in the name of Jesus.

PRAYERS TO DESTROY EVIL MARITAL YOKES

Song: By the reason of the anointing every yoke shall be broken.

1. Place your right hand on your head as you pray this prayer. Thou fire of God baptize me now.
2. Jesus the yoke breaker visit my life today.
3. Anointing that breaks the yoke of marital failure, come upon me in the name of Jesus.
4. Every power slowing down my marital progress, die by fire.
5. Unprofitable delay of my marital breakthroughs receive the consuming fire of God.
6. I bind and break every evil foundational yoke working against my life and marriage in the name of Jesus.
7. Every doorway and ladder of satanic invasion in my life, be abolished by the blood of Jesus.
8. Every placenta bondage tying me down to perpetual marital failure, break by fire in the name of Jesus.
9. Every yoke of marital delay, break and die, in Jesus name.
10. Any evil yoke waiting for my day of glory to manifest, die by fire.
11. Multiple problems in my marital life, break and die now.
12. I recover back the vehicle of my marriage from the hand of evil drivers, in the name of Jesus.
13. Vehicle of joy and glory, carry me to my divine destination.
14. Thank You Lord for breaking all the evil yokes limiting my life and marriage.

33. SPIRITUAL MARRIAGE

"There were giants in the earth in those days; and also after that, when the sons of God came in unto the daughters of men, and they bare children to them, the same became mighty men which were of old, men of renown." Genesis 6:4.

"For thou wilt not leave my soul in hell; neither wilt thou suffer thine Holy One to see corruption." Psalm 16:10.

A spiritual marriage is a marriage that exists in the spirit realm between a spirit being and human being. Spiritual marriages usually take precedence over physical marriages because the spiritual realm takes precedence over the physical. The male spirit being is known as incubus, while the female spirit being is known as succubus. These wicked spirit husbands and wives appear in the dream to sexually molest their victims. Some of the most stubborn and vicious spirit spouses are the marine spirit spouses, which come from the waters.

Spirit spouses leave evil deposits behind in their victims after having sex with them. These can cause a lot of problems spiritually and physically if not addressed properly. Spiritually; they bring pollution; spiritual weakness; loss of virtues; satanic delay; and the loss of good things. Physically, they lead to diseases and other medical problems such as fibroids, infertility, low sperm count, impotence, miscarriages, and still births.

Spirit spouses are very deceptive. They can lay dormant for a long time and then manifest and attack viciously when you pray targeted and hot prayers against them. This is to try to force you to stop praying the prayers. You must not give up but continue with the prayer program. They also manifest when there is a promising relationship in the horizon.

In the area of marriage, spirit spouse dreams can create problems in a promising marital relationship. These dreams include sex in the dream; having or breastfeeding babies; seeing yourself with a different spouse and children that are different from those that you have in real life; miscarriage of physical pregnancy after having intercourse in the dream; swimming in the water; seeing rings on your fingers; getting married in the dream; and breastfeeding babies.

Sex in the dream is often the weapon of stubborn, jealous, and vicious spirit spouses that want you to remain married to them. Sometimes sex in the dream is perpetuated by occult satanic agents moving about as men and women who use astral sex to harass people in their dreams. Say:

Satanic agents moving around as men and women, be exposed and disgraced in the mighty name of Jesus

Spirit spouses are clever spiritual thieves who steal people's virtues and testimonies. Their target is to keep the glory of God from manifesting in a person's life. They possess strong monitoring abilities and can sense when good things are coming your way. Then they show up with one agenda in mind which is to steal and abort the good thing.

Spirit spouses are very jealous and wicked. They launch vicious attacks to prevent their victims from getting married and having children in the physical realm because they want them to remain married to them. They terrorize the would-be earthly spouses of their victims, sometimes going as far as physically killing them. They terrorize through various tactics such as vicious attacks in the dream, accidents, poverty, embargo, and frustration. After sex with spirit spouses in the dream, a promising relationship often ends suddenly and disastrously.

Certain factors facilitate assault by spirit spouses. They act as door openers or satanic ladders for them to be able operate in a person's life. Such factors include wearing artificial human hair on your head. Another is wearing dreadlocks. Others are reading worldly books such as romance books; pornography; watching worldly and lewd movies, videos, or television programs; and wearing worldly exposing clothes and makeup. Another factor that can trigger the attacks is being in polluted, unclean spiritual environments such as polluted churches, fellowships, and private homes.

Sometimes spirit spouses use the faces of people that are very dear to a person to deceive the person into having sex with them in the dream. This includes the face of a brother, prospective partner, and deceased relatives such as a spouse, pastor, or even parents. We must not be ignorant of the devices of the devil in this area. **2 Corinthians 2:11.** In a new relationship they may take on the face of the new suitor.

Spirit spouses destroy your blessings by making your divine helpers look like your enemies and enemies to appear as friends. In fact, sometimes they may use the face of your pastor just to deceive you, so that you will leave the church where you are under divine protective covering and where you are receiving the spiritual help that you need to get victory over them. Once you leave the church, they then finish off your destiny. May we never be deceived by the devil in Jesus name! Say:

I will not be deceived by the devil, I will extol myself in the name of Jesus.

When the devil uses the face of a loved one to sexually molest you in your dream, you should refuse to be dejected. Do not let it ruin your day. Simply wake up, cancel the evil dream and its effects, pray cleansing prayers, anoint yourself with oil, drink some of anointing oil to destroy any evil deposit left behind by the wicked spirit spouse, and go about your business for the day. You should also take Holy Communion. Often the target of the "sex in the dream" strategy is the new thing that God is doing in your life. The agenda of the enemy is to abort it. So remember to cover and barricade these new things with the blood of Jesus and the fire of God always.

Recently, a sister came for one of our deliverance services where we ministered on the issue of spirit spouses. On getting home she went to bed as she normally did. Strangely when she woke up the following morning she saw a pair of man's socks lying on the floor besides her bed. That was the first time that she became aware that a spirit husband had been sleeping on her bed every night until that deliverance service where she was set free. Soon after that she met a brother who proposed marriage to her and she got married. Praise the Lord! God is faithful. To Him alone be all the glory! You are next in line for marriage in the name of Jesus. I say your miracle is already here in Jesus name.

DO IT RIGHT THIS TIME

PRAYERS FOR FREEDOM FROM EVIL SPIRITUAL MARRIAGE

Song: Shake! Shake! Shake! Shake the devil off.

1. Every stubborn spirit spouse claiming to be my spouse and saying that I cannot marry anyone else, you are a liar, fall down and die now.
2. You power of spirit spouse, I bury you today, in the mighty name of Jesus.
3. You demonic marriage, lose you hold over my life, in the name of Jesus.
4. Everything deposited in me by the spirit spouse that is working against my marriage, come out with all your roots and die, in Jesus name.
5. I drink the blood of Jesus and I swallow the fire of the Holy Ghost.
6. Holy Ghost fire purge my spirit, soul and body of every pollution.
7. Every owner of evil load of fibroid, appear and carry your load.
9. Blood of Jesus, release me from every evil marriage that is polluting my life and destiny.
10. Every spirit spouse, harassing my life, be castrated and die now. I cut off your manhood/womanhood with the sword of God, die now, in the name of Jesus. (*Imagine yourself holding a sword and using it to cut it off. Please take some time to pray this prayer and demonstrate it.*)
11. I break every blood and soul-tie covenant with all spirit spouses, by the blood of Jesus.
12. Every strange marriage preventing my physical marriage from manifesting, die.
13. Every satanic authority claiming ownership of my life, you are a liar, fall down and die, in the name of Jesus.
14. Powers from the waters attacking my marital destiny, your time is up, die by fire.
15. Evil marriage, I shake you out of my life, in the name of Jesus.

16. Every ancestral/generational spirit spouse militating against my marriage, release me and die now.

17. I issue a bill of divorcement to every spirit spouse laying claims of ownership upon my life.

18. I break all covenants entered into with spirit spouse by the power in the blood of Jesus.

19. I send the thunder fire of God to burn to ashes the children born to the marriage.

20. Evil wedding rings and garments, be roasted to ashes, in the name of Jesus.

21. Every astral projection against me, I frustrate you by the blood of Jesus.

22. Power of astral sex upon my life, die, in the name of Jesus.

23. Every power working against my marriage, fall down and die.

24. I purge out with the blood of Jesus every material deposited in my womb by spirit spouse to prevent me from having children for my earthly spouse.

25. I ordain a new time, season, and profitable law in Jesus name.

26. Every curse, bewitchment, incantation, and enchantment done against me by any spirit spouse, be reversed, by the blood of Jesus.

27. O Lord, restore all that any spiritual marriage has damaged, stolen, or destroyed in my life.

CHAPTER 12

BENEFITS OF DOING IT RIGHT THIS TIME

Please pray the following prayers:

1. Marital bliss locate me by fire in the name of Jesus.
2. O Lord, put love in my husband's heart for me, in the mighty name of Jesus.
3. O Lord stretch forth your hand from heaven and give me my own spouse, in the name of Jesus.
4. O Lord, please give me my own spouse in the name of Jesus.
5. Let my spouse, love me by fire, in the name of Jesus.

Doing it right means getting married the God prescribed way, to the God chosen person, and at the God appointed time. It means building the foundation of the marriage on Christ the Solid Rock. The result is a godly marital relationship that has several benefits. Some of these benefits are outlined in **Psalm 128** below. They include happiness, goodness, peace, fruitfulness, joy, and long life. We will be discussing these benefits below.

"Blessed is every one that feareth the LORD; that walketh in his ways. For thou shalt eat the labor of thine hands: happy shalt thou be, and it shall be well with thee. Thy wife shall be as a fruitful vine by the sides of thine house: thy children like olive plants round about thy table. Behold, that thus shall the man be blessed that feareth the LORD. The LORD shall bless thee out of Zion: and thou shalt see the good of Jerusalem all the days of thy life. Yea,

189

thou shalt see thy children's children, and peace upon Israel."
Psalm 128:1-6.

A marriage that is built on a strong Christian foundation will not collapse when the storms of life come. Instead it will stand because it is built on the word of God, the guidance of God, and it is the doing of the Holy Spirit. When the storms come, Jesus Christ, the Prince of Peace who resides in the house will simply say, "Peace, be still," and the storm will cease. The Bible talking of the durability of such a relationship says:

"Therefore whosoever heareth these sayings of mine, and doeth them, I will liken him unto a wise man, which built his house upon a rock: "And the rain descended, and the floods came, and the winds blew, and beat upon that house; and it fell not: for it was founded upon a rock. And every one that heareth these sayings of mine, and doeth them not, shall be likened unto a foolish man, which built his house upon the sand: And the rain descended, and the floods came, and the winds blew, and beat upon that house; and it fell: and great was the fall of it." Matthew 7:24-27.

YOU ENTER INTO THE REST OF GOD IN MARRIAGE

"Let us therefore fear lest a promise being left us of entering into his rest, any of you should seem to come short of it." Hebrews 4:1.

The Bible in several places talks about entering into the rest of God. This is a promise that God has made to His children if certain conditions are met. If we get married the God way this time around then we can expect to enter into His rest in the area of marriage.

What then is this rest? The rest of God means so many things. To enter the rest of God means that the season of laboring hard for your marital breakthrough are over and the season of harvest has come. It is now time for you to enjoy the fruits of your labor.

God started this pattern at creation by laboring for six days and resting on the seventh day. The seventh day is the day of completion, perfection, and fulfilment. It is the day of rest.

190

"And on the seventh day God ended his work which he had made; and he rested on the seventh day from all his work which he had made. And God blessed the seventh day, and sanctified it: because that in it he had rested from all his work which God created and made." Genesis 2:2-3.

"For He spake in a certain place of the seventh day in this wise. And God did rest the seventh day from all his works." (Hebrew 4:4).

It is the Sabbath day or Sunday for Christians. (Genesis 2:2-3).

For anyone seeking a godly spouse and marriage, entering into the rest of God connotes several things. We will now look at these below.

SEASON OF RESTORATION

The season of rest is the season when God remembers us and restores back to us what the devil has stolen from us or what we have lost through our own carelessness. It is the season when all the good things that the enemy has buried in our lives are exhumed and restored back to us. The Prophet Joel gives a very vivid picture of restoration in the scripture below:

"And I will restore to you the years that the locust hath eaten, the cankerworm, and the caterpillar, and the palmerworm, my great army which I sent among you. And ye shall eat in plenty, and be satisfied, and praise the name of the LORD your God that hath dealt wondrously with you: and my people shall never be ashamed. And ye shall know that I am in the midst of Israel, and that I am the LORD your God, and none else: and my people shall never be ashamed." Joel 2:25-27.

The season of restoration is the season when we get double blessings for all our shame.

"For your shame ye shall have double; and for confusion they shall rejoice in their portion: therefore in their land they shall possess the double: everlasting joy shall be unto them." Isaiah 61:7.

God knows how to give us double blessings for our shame and reproach. He knows how to make up for all the lost time. It is possible to be in a marriage for thirty years and never know joy, peace, or fulfillment. On the other hand, it is quite a different story when you do it right. It then becomes possible to be married for just one year and have so much peace, fulfillment, and joy that you forget all the years of pain, mockery, tears, shame, neglect, and rejection. That will be our portion this season in the mighty name of Jesus. Amen!

Fear not; for thou shalt not be ashamed: neither be thou confounded; for thou shalt not be put to shame: for thou shalt forget the shame of thy youth, and shalt not remember the reproach of thy widowhood any more. Isaiah 54:4.

SEASON OF GREAT HARVEST

It is a season when profitless hard work comes to an end and you stop working like an elephant and eating like an ant. It is when devourers, wasters, emptiers, spoilers, and other anti-harvest powers are arrested and you no longer labor in vain. It is when all your spiritual and physical investment in your marital destiny or even in a particular relationship begins to pay off. These investments include prayers; fasting; participating in deliverance programs; and confessions. All your work of faith pays off too. **James 2:26.** This includes buying things to be used for the wedding; buying gifts and cards and addressing them to your prospective spouse; buying clothes for the babies that you expect from the marriage; and other physical contributions such as telephone calls all pay off. It is a place where after much labor sowing and building, you reap marital bliss and fruitfulness. You no longer sow and others eat, devour, or spoil the fruit of your labor. You actually see the result of your labor and you eat of its fruit.

"For the LORD hath redeemed Jacob, and ransomed him from the hand of him that was stronger than he. Therefore they shall come and sing in the height of Zion, and shall flow together to the goodness of the LORD, for wheat, and for wine, and for oil, and for the young of the flock and of the herd: and their soul shall be as a watered garden; and they shall not sorrow any more at all. Then shall the virgin rejoice in the dance, both young men and old together: for I will turn their mourning into joy, and will comfort them, and make them rejoice from their sorrow. And I will satiate the soul of the priests with fatness, and my people shall be satisfied with my goodness, saith the LORD." Jeremiah 31:11-14.

SEASON OF FULFILLMENT

The season of rest is the morning of joy and fulfillment after the long night of sorrow, tears, frustrations, shame, and disappointments. We see this in the life of Isaac after Rebecca was brought to him as his wife. She met him sorrowful because of his mother's death but she consoled him and brought joy and fulfillment back into his life. **Genesis 24:67.**

It is a place of great satisfaction and deep personal fulfillment. Ruth must have enjoyed this kind of deep fulfillment when her situation turned around from widowhood and tears and she became the wife of Boaz.

SEASON OF GREAT JOY

The season of rest is the season of joy. If you know that your season of marital joy is here, join me in singing this song:

> I'm trading my sorrows
> I'm trading my shame
> I'm laying them down for the joy of the Lord
> I'm trading my sickness
> I'm trading my pain
> I'm laying it down for the joy of the Lord
> We say yes Lord yes Lord yes yes Lord
> Yes Lord yes Lord yes yes Lord
> Yes Lord yes Lord yes yes Lord Amen

> I'm pressed but not crushed persecuted not
> abandoned
> Struck down but not destroyed
> I am blessed beyond the curse for his promise
> will endure
> That his joy's gonna be my strength
> Though the sorrow may last for the night
> His joy comes with the morning

The season of joy is when your mourning turns into dancing and gladness. It is when your night turns to morning and your weeping turns to Joy as the psalmist says below:

"For his anger endureth but a moment; in his favor is life: weeping may endure for a night, but joy cometh in the morning." Psalm 30:5.

Today, I prophesy over you that your nights of weeping over your marital challenge are over. Your morning has come and with it your full joy in Jesus name. I prophesy over your marital life with the following song that your morning of joy and victory has come and it shall remain in Jesus name. If you believe it, then stand up and sing and dance with me as we sing:

> There is joy in the morning
> There is joy in the morning
> Child of God; weep no more
> There is joy in the morning
> (Repeat all over again)

SEASON OF LAUGHTER

The season of rest is the season of laughter like Abraham and Sarah laughed when their son Isaac finally came after years of waiting on the Lord to give them the promised son. God Himself named him "Isaac," meaning laughter. **Genesis 21:6.** Even today the season of great laughter has come to stay in your life, in the mighty name of Jesus. Amen! I decree over your life that this season many will hear your story and laugh with you in the mighty name of Jesus. Amen! On your wedding day and every day thereafter your joy will be so full that you shall sing:

> This is my day of joy
> My day of joy, my day of joy
> This is my day of joy, my day of joy, my day of joy
>
> This is my day of victory
> My day victory, my day of victory
> This is my day of victory, my day of victory, my day of victory

Yes! God indeed knows how to anoint us with oil of gladness above our fellows. **Psalm 45:7.** And this year He most certainly will in Jesus name.

PRAYERS

1. My marital joy and glory explode by fire, in the name of Jesus.
2. Every evil entity sitting on my marital glory summersault and die.
3. Every evil personality occupying my place in the life of my God ordained spouse, be unseated by fire, in the name of Jesus.
4. I claim and take back my rightful place, the name of Jesus.
5. This year my joy shall be full in the name of Jesus.

SEASON OF REMEMBRANCE

The season of rest is when God remembers you and intervenes in your situation. He takes away your sorrow, shame, and reproach. God remembered Hannah and made her an advertisement of His miracle working power. **1 Samuel chapters 1 and 2.** He did this by banishing barrenness and giving her a son, Samuel, who became renowned as one of the greatest prophets in the Bible. Not only that, God gave her five more children.

He remembered old, faithful, and childless Zacharias and Elizabeth and gave them a son, John, who became a forerunner of Christ. **Luke 1:13.** Our Lord Jesus described him as the greatest of all the Old Testament prophets. **Matthew 11:7-14.** Even so the Lord will remember and visit us this season, and grant us the desires of our hearts. He will give us our own spouses, children, and homes in Jesus name. Not only that, He will help us to build our homes and everlasting joy, fulfillment, and victory shall be our portion in Jesus name. Amen!!!

SEASON OF NEW SONG AND NEW DANCE

It is a season where new songs burst forth from your mouth in praise and awesome wonder in appreciation of what God has done and is doing in your marital life. It is also a season that you dance your new dance and write your new book out of gratitude to God. In 1994, when God rolled away the reproach of barrenness from my life all I could do was dance a new dance and sing a new song that simply said "Thank you Jesus," for over two hours nonstop. This season you shall sing your new song, dance your new dance, and write your new book in Jesus name.

PRAYERS

1. Every power that does not want me to sing my new song and dance my new dance in the area of marriage, fall down and die.
2. All anti-testimony forces working against my life and marriage, scatter by fire.

SEASON OF PEACE

The season of rest is the season peace because all the warfare that you fought before are gone. The boasting Goliaths that confronted your marital destiny have been disgraced and paralyzed. The stubborn Pharaoh pursuing you has drowned in his own Red Sea.

It is a place of tranquility such as prevailed in the life of King Solomon who took over from his father, David, as king in Israel. His father had fought all the wars and subdued all the enemies by the time he took over as king.

During Solomon's tenure as king peace reigned in the land. This made the environment conducive for the phenomenal growth and development that brought him international acclaim. **1 Chronicles 22:9.**

God indeed shall increase our greatness and comfort us on every side this season in Jesus name. **Psalm 71:21.** Our season of peace shall know no end in Jesus name.

SEASON OF TURN-AROUND BREAKTHROUGHS

"When the Lord brought back the captivity of Zion. We were like those who dream. Then our mouth was filled with laughter, and our tongue with singing. Then they said among the nations. "The Lord has done great things for us. And we are glad." Psalm 126:1-3.

It is the season that God turns around out captivity so that we are as those that dream as the psalmist says above. It is a season of turnaround breakthroughs in which God turns our marital mess into a message of bliss. All the past rejection turns to love and acceptance and all the disappointments turn to favor. Whereas before there were no suitors, now we have a new problem of choosing the right one out of many suitors.

Remember Ruth? She forgot the reproach of her widowhood when she met and married Boaz, her kinsman redeemer. She not only found love, care, and affluence, but she became the mother of Obed, who was an ancestor of our Lord Jesus. All her tears turned to joy. See what the Bible says about her turnaround testimony:

"So Boaz took Ruth, and she was his wife: and when he went in unto her, the Lord gave her conception, and she bare a son. And the women said unto Naomi, Blessed be the Lord, which hath not left thee this day without a kinsman, that his name may be famous in Israel. And he shall be unto thee a restorer of thy life, and a nourisher of thine old age: for thy daughter in law, which loveth thee, which is better to thee than seven sons, hath born him." Ruth 4:13-15.

DO IT RIGHT THIS TIME

I prophesy that the time to favor you matrimonially is here in the mighty name of Jesus. Do you see everything turning around for your marital breakthroughs? Do you see everything working in your favor? If yes, then sing this chorus with me as you prophetically dance your way into your marital breakthrough:

> **I can see everything turning around**
> **O yea yea turning around**
> **O yea yea turning around**
> **In my favor (break-through)**
>
> **I can see everything turning around**
> **O yea yea turning around**
> **O yea yea turning around**
> **In my favor (break-through)**

I see our marital lives turning around for good this season, in the mighty name of Jesus. If you believe so shout, "Amen! Amen!! And Amen!!!"

SEASON OF LATTER RAIN BLESSING

The season of rest is the season of the latter rain. It is when you not only get the former rain but also the latter rain which is an extra blessing.

"Be glad then, ye children of Zion, and rejoice in the LORD your God: for he hath given you the former rain moderately, and he will cause to come down for you the rain, the former rain, and the latter rain in the first month." Joel 2:23.

This was the case with Job who had lost everything that he had. He lost children, wealth, health, honor and esteem, and possessions. At the end of the affliction, he got back everything that he had lost in multiples. You too will get back all that God has ordained for you in the area of marriage, including everything that the enemy has stolen from you.

"Now the Lord blessed the latter days of job more that his beginning." Job 42:12-13.

Perhaps, you have tried marriage before but it ended in disaster, a broken heart, bruised emotions, rejection, and abandonment. Having been burned once, you have waited patiently for the Lord to help you to do it right this time. Your patience will pay off because, this season, you will receive the former and the latter rain in your marriage:

"Be patient therefore, brethren, unto the coming of the Lord. Behold, the husbandman waiteth for the precious fruit of the earth, and hath long patience for it, until he receive the early and latter rain." James 5:7.

Today, the God of the suddenly is showing up in your situation. Through this book, He is giving you the opportunity for a new beginning. You may have lost many battles but you will win the war raging over your marital destiny in the name of Jesus. That husband will locate you now by fire. That wife is here already. That wonderful home that you have been dreaming about, receive it. Receive your children, in the name of Jesus.

Always keep in mind that the Bible says better is the end of a thing than the beginning. What do you hear? I hear the sound of the abundance of rain. It is here to pour on and refresh your marital destiny. Your expectations will not be cut off in Jesus name. With a heart of thanksgiving for this rain, let us sing unto our God with great anticipation:

> **Thank you for the rain**
> **Thank you for the latter rain**
> **Healing the sick**
> **Confirming your words**
> **Thank you for the latter rain**
>
> **(Thank you Thank you daddy)**
> **Thank you for the rain**
> **Thank you for the latter rain**
> **Healing the sick**

> Confirming your words
> Thank you for the latter rain

In our incredible joy and victory we will sing also with gratitude this song:

> It is raining all over me
> I can feel it
> It is a lot of rain
> Come Lord Jesus
> Send us more rain
> Until we are filled,
> Until we are soaked with the latter rain

GODLY CHILDREN

When we get married in the right way the promises of God in the Bible automatically pursue us. One such promise is that we will bear children.

"Lo, children are an heritage of the Lord: and the fruit of the womb is his reward." Psalm 127:3.

This is guaranteed us even in our old age.

"Those that be planted in the house of the Lord shall flourish in the courts of our God. They shall still bring forth fruit in old age; they shall be fat and flourishing; Psalm 92:13-14.

Sarah and Abraham had Isaac in their old age. **Genesis 21:1-7.** Job's wife, in her season of restoration, had ten more children after she lost her original set of children to disaster. **Job 42:12-15.**

In the book of Malachi, we are further promised that such children will be godly:

"Yet she is your companion and your wife by covenant. But did He not make them one, Having a remnant of the Spirit? And why one?

200

He seeks godly offspring. Therefore take heed to your spirit, and let none deal treacherously with the wife of his youth. Malachi 2:14-15."

We can also stand on **Isaiah 1:18** and claim not just godly but Holy Ghost filled children that are for signs and wonders in their generation:

"Behold, I and the children whom the LORD hath given me are for signs and for wonders in Israel from the LORD of hosts, which dwelleth in Zion."

If you are thinking "I am old and I have hit menopause so it is too late to have children," then remember Sarah and Abraham who had Isaac at age 90 and 100 respectively. We have them for our example. Keep reminding God of this and you read **Psalm 92** quoted above often so that it can sink into your spirit and claim the promise of fruitfulness therein.

"Those that be planted in the house of the LORD shall flourish in the courts of our God. They shall still bring forth fruit in old age; they shall be fat and flourishing" Psalm 92:13-14.

Regardless of your age, regardless of "menopause", you shall not only get married but you shall have as many children as God has ordained for you in the mighty name of Jesus. Not only that, God will give you the long life and good health to enjoy them as He did for Job. **Job 42:12-17.**

When people think or say "you cannot have children," it is then God steps in and says "you can". This is because there are no impossibilities with God. **Luke 18:27**. He can do whatever He chooses to do whenever He chooses to do it. Menopause cannot stop you as God is able to reduce your age to bring His divine purpose in your life to pass. Receive the miracle of age reduction in Jesus name. Receive the miracle of having children when everyone has written you off in the name of Jesus. If you belief this, please make the following confessions 21 times loud and clear:

"The joy and fulfillment of child bearing is mine, in Jesus name."

"The victory of suckling my own children is mine in Jesus name."

DO IT RIGHT THIS TIME

PRAYERS TO PROTECT THE GODLY SEED IN ME

Song: My marriage shall be a blessing
My children around my table
I shall see my children's children
Thus saith the living God

1. Powers assigned to kill the godly seed in me and my divine partners' loins, fail and die.

2. Any power that has swallowed up my God assigned seed, burst open, vomit it now, and die.

3. My womb, reject every seed of miscarriage and abortion of goodness, in the name of Jesus.

4. Every power that has programmed evil, tragedy, and untimely death into the lives of the godly seed that God has ordained from my marriage, you are a failure, die now.

5. Every spirit of sickness, birth defects, untimely death, tragedy, and other evil things programmed to manifest in the lives of the children that God has ordained from my marriage, die now.

6. Every evil clock and calendar constructed for my future God ordained children, catch fire and be destroyed now.

7. Evil hands working against the goodness of my God ordained children, wither and die.

8. My children shall be a blessing to their generation, in the name of Jesus.

DIVORCE PROOF MARRIAGE

"For the Lord God of Israel says that He Hates divorce For it covers one's garment with violence." Says the Lord of hosts "therefore take heed to your spirit, that you do not deal treacherously." Malachi 2:16.

One of the benefits of doing it right this time is that you get a divorce proof marriage. You can be sure that even when you get married the right way, the storms will still come because satan does not like good things. Regardless of this, a godly marriage will stand and not collapse because the foundation is built on the only sure Rock, Jesus Christ. **1 Corinthians 3:11.** When the storms come, the anchor will hold. It will not be like the house built on sand that collapses when it comes under pressure. **Mathew 7:26.** When people around you are running to get a divorce, the difference will be very clear as you rest assured that your anchor holds and cannot fail. You should remind yourself of this often as you sing like job did in **Job 19:25,** the following song:

> I know my redeemer liveth
> Yes I know my Redeemer liveth
> Yes I know my Redeemer He liveth
> He liveth forever more

You can sing the following song also:

> Let the redeemed of the Lord say so
> Let the redeemed of the Lord say so
> Let the redeemed of the Lord say so
> I am redeemed I am redeemed
> Praise the Lord!

PRAYERS TO DIVORCE PROOF YOUR MARRIAGE

1. Any power that wants to make my marital destiny a grave yard, die now.

2. Every power of my father's house that has vowed that I will not secure a place in and remain in the company of the married, fail and die.

3. Every power of my mother's house that has vowed that I will not secure a place in and remain in the school of the married, fail and die.

4. Every platform of divorce prepared for my marital destiny, I pull you down, perish by fire, in the name of Jesus.

5. Every evil prophesy, pronouncement, and judgment of divorce spoken over my life and marital destiny, be nullified by the blood of Jesus.

6. Every evil covenant keeping divorce in place in my life, break by the blood of Jesus.

7. Every evil tongue speaking divorce over my marital destiny, wither and be cut off.

8. Every power, personality, or spirit programming divorce into my marital destiny, you are a liar, die now.

9. Every arrow of divorce fired into my marital destiny, backfire.

10. Every owner of evil load of divorce, carry your load and go.

11. Every evil ordination, verdict, and decree of divorce for my life, be overturned by the blood of Jesus.

12. Every power, personality, and spirit working against my marital wellbeing, fall down and die in the name of Jesus.

13. I paralyze all evil legs and hands moving about for the sake of my marriage, in the name of Jesus.

14. Evil hands militating against my settling down in marriage, wither, and be cut off in the name of Jesus.

15. Every evil pattern of ancestral loneliness and divorce of my father's house break and release me in the name of Jesus.

16. Every evil pattern of divorce of my mother's house, be de-patterned by the blood of Jesus.

17. Every garment of shame and reproach prepared for my marriage, catch fire and burn to ashes, in Jesus name.

18. I refuse to pay for what I did not buy in the name of Jesus.

19. Every power that wants me to pay for what I did not buy, release me and die.

20. Every evil altar and priest launching attacks against my getting married and staying married, die by fire.

YOU GET A WISE AND RESOURCEFUL WIFE

You get a woman who is the bone of your bone and the flesh of your flesh. She is the only one in the universe that the Lord has prepared and equipped just for you. She understands how you are wired because she is the one that was taken from your rib, just like Eve, the first wife, was taken out of her husband Adam's rib. This is the woman that God has ordained and equipped from the beginning to complement and bring you fulfillment. You may be very different in personality and other ways but she is your help mate. She has been imbued and endued with the qualities and virtues that will please you and keep you fulfilled so that the desire to go outside will not even be there. Physically, she will be a delight. Mentally, you will find her challenging. Emotionally, she will be fulfilling to you.

In the vineyard of the Lord, she will be your helper. Every day, she will bring fresh ideas. She will not duplicate your ideas. Rather being a handmaiden of God, who waits on Him continuously, she will bring you fresh revelations from His presence. She will positively impact every area of your life and move the home, business, career, and calling forward.

In conclusion, she is not stale, her ideas are not stale, and her looks are not stale. She stays attached to the socket of the almighty and to the fresh moving water of the Holy Spirit. She partakes daily of the fragrance of Jesus which she brings daily into the relationship. Daily, she is fresh, beautiful, attractive, and resourceful.

Recognizing all the virtues mentioned above, the Bible queries in **Proverbs 31**, "Who can find a virtuous woman?" Who indeed can find a virtuous woman? Yet God being a wonderful Father has handpicked one for you as His beloved son. Brothers know for sure that you are blessed if you have found her! Therefore, appreciate her, honor her, and cherish her. She is a gift to you from God. Enjoy her!!!!!

"Who can find a virtuous woman? for her price is far above rubies. The heart of her husband doth safely trust in her, so that he shall have no need of spoil. She will do him good and not evil all the days of her life. She seeketh wool, and flax, and worketh willingly with her hands. She is like the merchants' ships; she bringeth her food from afar. She riseth also while it is yet night, and giveth meat to her household, and a portion to her maidens. She considereth a field, and buyeth it: with the fruit of her hands she planteth a vineyard. She girdeth her loins with strength, and strengtheneth her arms. She perceiveth that her merchandise is good: her candle goeth not out by night. She layeth her hands to the spindle, and her hands hold the distaff. She stretcheth out her hand to the poor; yea, she reacheth forth her hands to the needy. She is not afraid of the snow for her household: for all her household are clothed with scarlet. he maketh herself coverings of tapestry; her clothing is silk and purple. Her husband is known in the gates, when he sitteth among the elders of the land. She maketh fine linen, and selleth it; and delivereth girdles unto the merchant. Strength and honour are her clothing; and she shall rejoice in time to come. She openeth her mouth with wisdom; and in her tongue is the law of kindness. She looketh well to the ways of her household, and eateth not the bread of idleness. Her children arise up, and call her blessed; her husband also, and he praiseth her. Many daughters have done virtuously, but thou excellest them all. Favour is deceitful, and beauty is vain: but a woman that feareth the LORD, she shall be praised. Give her of the fruit of her hands; and let her own works praise her in the gates." Proverbs 31:10-31.

AN HONORABLE AND DISTINGUISHED SPOUSE

Marriage brings honor when you do it the right way. As a woman, you get a husband that is honored at the gate.

"Her husband is known in the gates, when he sitteth among the elders of the land." Proverbs 31:23.

The gate is where you find the influential people in any community. It is the seat of power where important decisions are made. This means that you get a man of substance, a man of integrity and power, who is respected and honored in his generation. You get a husband who is the head and not the tail. He is able to carry his responsibility in the home, in the body of Christ, and in the larger community. You get a matured man who is able and willing to shoulder his responsibilities at all three levels, and not an immature boy.

As a man, you get a wife that is that is robed in honor and strength.

"Strength and honor are her clothing; and she shall rejoice in time to come." Proverbs 31:25.

PROSPERITY

"Beloved, I wish above all things that thou mayest prosper and be in health, even as thy soul prospereth." 3 John 1:2.

"Blessed is the man that walketh not in the counsel of the ungodly, nor standeth in the way of sinners, nor sitteth in the seat of the scornful. But his delight is in the law of the Lord; and in his law doth he meditate day and night. And he shall be like a tree planted by the rivers of water, that bringeth forth his fruit in his season; his leaf also shall not wither; and whatsoever he doeth shall prosper." Psalm 1:1-3.

Prosperity simply means that you eat the good of the land if you are willing and obedient to God in picking a spouse. **Isaiah 1:9.** Being willing and obedient means that you choose to get a spouse the right way this time around by following the principles of God laid down in the Bible in locating your partner, in courtship and in getting married. These principles are clearly explained in this marriage manual.

"This book of the law shall not depart out of thy mouth; but thou shalt meditate therein day and night, that thou mayest observe to do according to all that is written therein: for then thou shalt make thy way prosperous, and then thou shalt have good success." Joshua 1:8.

It means that you choose not to do it your own way or in the way that the people of this world around you do it. It is a conscious decision not to engage in all the heavy petting; sex before marriage, the frolicking; the going into relationships for selfish reasons instead of in obedience to God's will and for love. It also entails choosing your friends carefully and staying away from bad company that can pull you away from God and His godly ways and towards the ways and the things of this world which are ungodly and unprofitable.

The Bible says that we should seek first the kingdom of God and His righteousness and *these other things* will be added onto us. **Matthew 6:33.** Therefore, if we go about our marriage the kingdom way, then we get in return all the added on blessings. Prosperity is one of the added on blessings mentioned above. This is our kingdom right as bona-fide members of God's kingdom who are living by the tenets of the kingdom.

YOU FORM A FORMIDABLE TEAM

"Two are better than one; because they have a good reward for their labour. For if they fall, the one will lift up his fellow: but woe to him that is alone when he falleth; for he hath not another to help him up. Again, if two lie together, then they have heat: but how can one be warm alone? And if one prevail against him, two shall withstand him; and a threefold cord is not quickly broken." Ecclesiastes 4:9-12.

When two people come together as husband and wife, they form a formidable team. The Bible says that one will chase a thousand and two ten thousand so even your prayer life is more effective. **Deuteronomy 32:30.**

From the scripture from Ecclesiastes quoted above, we can see that there are several reasons for this. One reason is that there is strength in numbers because two are better than one. Another is that if one of them falls then the other one will help get him back on his feet. Yet another is that a threefold cord is not easily broken. The bond between you, your partner, and God becomes this three-fold cord. The Bible also says that iron sharpens iron. **Proverbs 27:17.** This means that you complement each other and bring out the best in one another. You get good counsel and a counselor that you can trust.

Therefore in a good marriage, you get a companion who shares your burden and a helper that helps you in various areas of life such as ministry, business, and raising children. You come out as one strong voice against the whole world. You have an ally to back you up at all times.

You are assured that your husband being a godly and God fearing man will not hurt you. You are also confident that he will obey the word of God and love his wife as Christ loved His church and gave His life for it. **Ephesians 5:25.** Marriage makes both of you one, so hurting your partner is tantamount to hurting your own self.

PRAYERS TO SAY BYE BYE TO SINGLENESS

Note: *All the prayers in this section should be prophetically demonstrated with great aggression.*

Song: **Bye bye to singleness o.**

1. I wave bye bye to singleness forever, in the name of Jesus. (Prophetically wave good bye as you sing the prayer song above).
2. I stand on the authority of the name and the blood of Jesus and I declare that the days of singleness are over in my life forever in the wonderful name of Jesus.
3. God, arise and let all the enemies of my peace and my joy, scatter, in the name of Jesus.
4. You my "Sunday", my day of marital rest, your time has come. *Appear now, appear by fire.* (Repeat over and over again "Appear now, appear by fire.")
5. I take off my old bed sheet and put on a fresh one, in preparation for the coming of my God ordained spouse. (Prophetically carry out this divine assignment by replacing the old bed sheet on your bed with a brand new one that has never before been used).
6. By the power of the Holy Ghost, I freshen up my marital bed, awaiting the visitation of my God ordained spouse.
7. You, my God ordained spouse, hear the word of the living God, the season of my marital rest is now here, therefore *appear now and take your place* on the marital bed that has been prepared for you, in the name of Jesus. (Repeat over and over "Appear now and take your place.")
8. By the power in the blood of Jesus, I prophesy over my life that this year I (put your name here) shall be married, in the name of Jesus.

9. Lord, this year by all the power by which you are known as the living God, relocate me to the school of the married after the order of Rebekah, the wife of Isaac, in the name of Jesus.

10. Holy Spirit, prepare, equip, and empower me to take my place effectively among the school of the married, in Jesus name.

11. Holy Spirit, arise and arrest every spirit of lateness of my marital goodness.

12. Every power, personality, or spirit occupying my God assigned place in the school of the married, vacate it, turn around, and get out.

13. My season of laboring over my marriage is over. Now, I enter into my season of marital rest, reward, joy, peace, and fulfillment, in Jesus name. (Prophetically demonstrate this by getting up and walking into your season of rest and fulfillment).

14. Lord, restore all my wasted years in the mighty name of Jesus.

15. Lord, arise and pour upon my head the oil of marital joy, gladness, and fulfillment in the name of Jesus.

16. Oh Lord, arise and change my story. Give me your ordained spouse for me today in the mighty name of Jesus.

17. Oh God of the suddenlies, turn my marital situation around today to favor me in the name of Jesus.

18. I prophesy over my life, that my appointed time, the season to favor me has come, in Jesus name.

19. I wave good bye to singleness in the name of Jesus.

20. I bulldoze my way into the company of the married by the power in the blood of Jesus.

CHAPTER 13

WORDS OF CAUTION FOR A GODLY RELATIONSHIP

ESCHEW DESPERATION

Do not be desperate to get married. It is better to remain single and have your peace than to push your way into a bad marriage and end up crying every day. We should take the time to get to know our proposed spouse before we go into any marriage. There should be no attempt to deceive ourselves, make excuses, and cut corners. By this I mean that you should not deliberately ignore all the tell-tale signs and evidence of things that could be problematic in the relationship later just because you desperately want to get married. You will only live to regret it if out of desperation, you deliberately ignore obvious signs such as callousness; heartlessness; wickedness; lack of love and compassion; selfishness; cruelty; arrogance; infidelity; and other bad traits. The leopard cannot change its spots as most people are already set in their ways by the time they marry.

Once you get into the marriage you will be faced with the reality of the situation and no excuses and delusion will help you at that time. It would be too late by then. Once again, let me emphasis that it is actually better to be single and have peace than to be in a troubled marriage. Many have learnt this lesson the hard way. So please look before you leap.

These words of caution are particularly important for those who have failed in marriage before and are getting married again. An old English adage says "Once bitten, twice shy." Therefore, there is need to

212

exercise great caution as statistics show that about 60% of all second marriages end up in divorce like the first one. If you fail this time around, your destiny may never recover from it so endeavor to do it right this time around. The Lord will empower you to do it right this time as you cling to Him in Jesus name. His grace is sufficient for you. **2 Corinthians 12:9.** Receive the grace to do it right this time in Jesus name.

DO NOT MARRY IN RESPONSE TO PHYSICAL NEEDS

Everything that God created has a divine purpose. Marriage is no different. God ordained the institution of marriage as a means of fulfilling a divine purpose so it is not an end by itself. Your marital destiny should align with God's assignment for your life. This means that your marriage should be a means of fulfilling a divine purpose first and foremost, and not to satisfy your physical needs. Therefore, you should first find out what your divine assignment is and then ensure that your marriage is in line with it.

Also, marriage is a spiritual transaction so it should be first on a spiritual level before being on a physical level. It involves a man and a woman being knitted together first spiritually and then physically. **Ephesians 5:28-33; 1 Corinthians 6:15-16.**

The Bible advices us to seek first the kingdom of God and His righteousness and then all other things that we need will be added unto us. **Matthew 6:33.** Our physical needs fall into the category of the "other things" that are added. They are the icing on the cake. As we seek first to fulfill the purpose of God for our marriage, the physical needs are met.

It should not be the other way around. You do not marry because you want your physical needs met. You should first ensure that that the marriage aligns with God's purpose for your life and that He approves the relationship. It is only then that you should get married. Of course, as mentioned above, as a result of the marriage your physical needs will end up being met as well. Loneliness will ease. Finances will get better due to the pooling of resources.

Why not ask the Lord today the divine purpose that your marriage should fulfill? Please do so before you enter any marriage.

STAY UNDER AUTHORITY

You should not try to beat or outwit the process laid down by divine authority in the Bible or by ministers that God has vested with spiritual authority over your life. You should not try to cut corners either as it will be to your own detriment.

It is actually in your best interest to adhere to the rules and regulations laid down by your church to guide their members in getting married in the biblical way. They are normally put in place to protect church members from being hurt and taken advantage of by unscrupulous people. They also act as checks and balances to prevent them from making serious mistakes that can destroy their destinies. Therefore, you will only be hurting yourself if you maneuver them to suit your own personal and often selfish needs. Instead, you should allow these checks and balances to serve their purpose. If they require that you wait for at least six months to get married so you can know yourselves better, then do so. If they say that you should not to visit each other's house unchaperoned then obey. Keep in mind that only the obedient gets to eat the good of the land. **Isaiah 1:19.**

In making decisions, you should realize that these rules are put there to help you lay a godly foundation for your marriage, home, and generations of children yet unborn. Without a solid foundation, sorrow and tears will surely be waiting on the other side of the door. The marital bliss and union of the spirit that God originally ordained for marriage will be far away then. I pray that this will not be your portion in Jesus name.

BEWARE OF EVIL COUNSELORS

Beware of evil "counselors" who pretend to be on your side by encouraging you to break church rules by making statements such as "You love each other, why wait for six months to get married?" and "You plan to get married so it is okay to sleep in his house." When your marriage turns sour and your life becomes a living hell, they will not be there to cry with you. You will be left there alone holding the shattered pieces. May that never be your portion in the name of Jesus.

BE ACCOUNTABLE

Get a proper spiritual cover and stay under it. It can save your life! Stay under the proper covering provided by those that God has put in authority over you. These include parental authority or church authority.

If your pastor says you cannot marry a person then take time to seek the Lord to know why he said so and to know the way forward. Most of the time, it is because they can see what you cannot see or they know things that you do not know. Do not just brush them aside and do what you want. God is not the author of confusion. There should be order in the house of God. Your pastor is the shepherd and you are the sheep. **Romans 13:1-4.** God made him or her shepherd over your life for a purpose. Do not frustrate that purpose. Please stay under cover. There are wolves and lions out there waiting to devour. They are inside the church as well. Do not allow yourself to become meat for them to devour.

If your parents disapprove of your marriage then you should ask God to intervene and pray until they come around before you get married. Parental blessing is very important in a marriage.

I know a sister that her church and her family opposed her getting married to a man. He claimed to be born again but possessed none of the fruits of a genuine child of God. The Lord warned the sister that she was treading a dangerous road, one that was full of deadly snakes. The sister, however, would not receive the warning and went ahead with the marriage. In her desperation to get married, she abandoned her home church that had her interest at heart and went to a strange church, where they did not know her and asked no questions, to marry the man. In the end he turned out to be a thief, an adulterer, and pedophile.

You see God cannot be mocked. The Bible admonishes us to be as wise as serpents and as gentle as doves. We should however not be wise in our own conceit. **Proverbs 26:12.** Whatever a man sows, is what he reaps. **Galatians 6:7.** You get to lie on your bed the way that you made it.

Despite godly counsel, another sister thought that it was okay to continue spending weekends with and sleeping with a man with whom she had a baby out of wedlock. She circulated his name to all sorts of satanic centers and intermediaries in a bid to manipulate him into marrying her. Even if the man does eventually marry her, the foundation of such a marriage is already terribly polluted. It would take the grace of God for that kind of a marriage to work or be fulfilling. It is one thing to get married but it is another thing to enjoy it and be fulfilled. We should do it right this time. As we do, marital bliss will be ours, in Jesus name.

A brother obviously ignorant of the fact that God has promised that judgment would start from His house, targeted the single ladies with stable income and profitable employment in a church. He told each of them that she was God's chosen marital partner for him. He eventually succeeded in marrying one of them. The only problem is that the bed of roses that he had schemed for and expected turned out to be a bed of thorns. It was a marriage made in hell from day one, with the police being called to settle fights often. Needless to say the marriage ended disastrously.

You should beware as the Bible says that God cannot be mocked. It goes further to say that we cannot hide anything from God:

"He that planted the ear, shall he not hear? He that formed the eye, shall he not see......he that teacheth man knowledge shall he not know?" Psalm 94:9.

Sometime ago, a brother in the church kept inviting himself to my house. I kept putting him off politely. Then I started dreaming about dogs. In one of the dreams, I cut off the head of the dog with a sword. After dealing with the situation in the spiritual realm, the brother came again. This time, I confronted him in the physical. I pointed out to him that our church policies do not permit men to visit single ladies alone. I later learnt that he was a habitual and unrepentant womanizer.

We must take a stand. We may be single but we are not desperate. At the right time God will perfect everything that pertains to our marriage. He will make all things indeed beautiful in His time. He is the pillar that holds our lives together. Know for sure that when you give Him your life He will never let you down. He will turn your marital mess into a marvelous message of marital victory and fulfillment for the whole world to read. Let us reinforce these truth by singing the following choruses together.

216

LORD I GIVE YOU MY LIFETIME

My life time
Lord I give you my lifetime
My life time
Lord I give you my lifetime
Because I've given you my lifetime
You will take care of me
You will never, never let me down
Because I have given you my lifetime

JESUS THE PILLAR THAT HOLDS MY LIFE

You are the Pillar that holds my life (together)
You are the Pillar that holds my life
Master Jesus
You are the pillar that holds my life
Master Jesus
You are the pillar that holds my life

HE MAKES ALL THINGS BEAUTIFUL IN HIS TIME

In His time
In His time
He makes all things so beautiful
In His time
Lord please show me everyday
As you are teaching me your way
That you do just what you say
In your time
In your time
In your time
You make all things so beautiful
In your time
Lord, my life to you I bring
May each song I have to sing
Be to you a lovely song
In your time

CHAPTER 14

CONCLUSION

As far as marriage is concerned, it is possible to do it right this time by marrying the God chosen person, in the biblical way, and at the God ordained time. This is because we can do all things through Christ. Also His grace is sufficient for us in any situation that life brings our way. **2 Corinthians 12:9.** To do it right this time, we have to be doers of the word and not just hearers only. We should seek God's face regularly and passionately through violent prayers and fasting to enable us know His will for us in marriage and to obtain continuous guidance throughout out the marriage process.

The word of God and the Holy Spirit must be involved in the process of doing it right this time. Prayer is a master key in doing it right this time. You should pray against powers that are opposed to your getting married and that want to keep you away from your God ordained spouse. You should pray for the Holy Spirit to bring you and your partner together and to glue you together in such a way that nothing and no one can separate you.

It is equally important that we also look at the other side of the coin by counting the cost of not doing it right this time.

It does not matter what our past marital experience has been, God is equipping us through this book to do it right this time around. Not only that, He will also make available to us new opportunities to do so. Today is the day of our salvation. **2 Corinthians 6:2.** There is yet hope for us. We can do it right this time, and reap the reward of doing it God's way which is peace, joy, fruitfulness, fulfillment, progress, promotion, and prosperity.

On the other hand, if we choose to continue doing things in the same ungodly ways that we have always done them, then the relationship will be fraught with massive storms, sorrow, barrenness, unfulfillment, failure, rejection, and defeat. These problems will fester and allow unforgiveness, frustration, bitterness, and malice to come into the home. Ultimately, the result will be strife, hindered prayers, lack of progress, and even untimely death.

Consequently, we will fail to achieve the purpose for which God instituted marriage as instead of His intended marital bliss, we will get gross unhappiness; instead of oneness and unity, we will get division and strife; instead of friendship we will get enmity; instead of trust, we will get suspicious; and instead of companionship, we will get loneliness and apathy. If left unchecked, this will eventually lead to separation and divorce.

The most devastating consequence of all is that instead of the godly children that God has promised as a fruit from a godly marriage, we may end up with dysfunctional children. This in turn will lay a foundation for trans-generational evil patterns to thrive in the family.

Armed with this book, which is a manual on getting married God's way, let us now do it in the way that God has set forth in His word, the Holy Bible. As we do this, our joy will be full in Jesus name. His grace will see us through in Jesus name.

Now sing this chorus with me if you believe that God who has started the good work in your marital life will be faithful to complete it at HIS appointed time and in HIS own special way:

HE WHO STARTED THE WORK

<u>CHORUS</u>
He who began a good work in you
He who began a good work in you
Will be faithful to complete it
He'll be faithful to complete it
He who started the work
Will be faithful to complete it in you

If the struggle you're facing
Is slowly replacing your hope
With despair
Or the process is long
And you're losing your song
In the night
You can be sure that the Lord
Has His hand on you
Safe and secure
He will never abandon you
You are His treasure
And He finds His pleasure in you

FATHER PERFECT YOUR WORK IN MY LIFE

You have been doing your work
Father perfect your work
You have been doing your work in my life
Father perfect your work

APPENDIX 1

STEPS TO SALVATION

1. Realize that all have sinned. (Romans 3:23)
2. Repent of all your sins. (Psalm 32:5, 1 John 1:8-9).
3. Confess all your known sins. (Acts 10:43).
4. Open the door of your heart so that Jesus can come in. (Revelation 3:20).
5. Ask the Lord Jesus Christ to come into your heart as your personal Lord and Savior. (John 1:12)
6. Confess that the Lord Jesus Christ is your Lord and Savior. (Romans 10:10).
7. Believe that you now have a new life in Christ Jesus and walk daily in that newness.

As you experience this newness in Christ and walk this new walk with Him, may you continuously hold His hand and walk with Him. May the Grace of our Lord Jesus Christ be with and keep and preserve you until His coming in Jesus name.

CALL: (281) 965-6727

FOR

COUNSELING

&

SINGLES DELIVERANCE

&

SINGLES SEMINARS

ABOUT THE AUTHOR

Pastor Morayo Isi, currently resides and pastors in the United States of America. She is the President of Royal House Ministries, Daughters of Zion, International, Arise School of Healing, and Agape Training Institute (U.S.A.). Her ministry and calling are anchored on two key scriptures: *Isaiah 61:1-2 and John 14:12.*

Pastor Morayo is a teacher, prophet, and intercessor. She is also actively involved in the ministry of deliverance. She believes strongly that deliverance is the heartbeat of the Almighty God for the world today. She is a living testimony of what the power of God can do.

In addition, she has been given a divine mandate to minister healing to God's people. She holds her quarterly "I Believe in Divine Healing," meetings and seminar on herbs, all over the world.

Pastor Morayo is available to teach, preach, and minister locally and internationally. She can help you write your own story. She can be reached by mail at: P.O. Box 420756 Houston, TX 77242, by email at morayoisi@royalhouseministries.org, and by phone at (281) 965-7627. You can access her articles at www.deliverancewithmorayo.blogspot.com.

DO IT RIGHT THIS TIME